Misreading Reading

THE BAD SCIENCE THAT HURTS CHILDREN

Gerald Coles

HEINEMANN
Portsmouth, NH

Heinemann
A division of Reed Elsevier Inc.
361 Hanover Street
Portsmouth, NH 03801–3912
www.heinemann.com

Offices and agents throughout the world

Library of Congress Cataloging-in-Publication
Coles, Gerald.
    Misreading reading : the bad science that hurts children / Gerald Coles.
       p.   cm.
    Includes bibliographical references and index.
    ISBN 0–325–00060–3
    1. Reading—Research. 2. Reading—Phonetic method—Research. 3. Reading—Language experience approach—Research.   I. Title.
LB1050.6.C65 2000
428'.4'072—dc21   99-055073

Editor: Lois Bridges
Production: Vicki Kasabian
Cover design: Michael Leary Design
Manufacturing: Deanna Richardson

Printed in the United States of America on acid-free paper
03 02 01 00 99 DA 1 2 3 4 5

To Milt and Bernice Schwebel,

extraordinary partisans for a world of justice, equality,
peace, and love

Contents

Acknowledgments

The regular, often daily, communication between my editor, Lois Bridges, and me (thanks to wondrous e-mail) is a measure of our working relationship and her contribution to this book. Beyond my appreciation of her superb editorial help and encouragement, however, I extend my gratitude for her own unflagging work on behalf of children's literacy education. To have an editor who not only talks the talk but walks the walk is rare!

Walking the walk also describes countless educators in public schools and universities across the United States and other countries who have struggled against the damaging education fostered by the bad science discussed in this book. I thank them for their efforts, inspiration, and camaraderie. Without them, there would have been little point in writing this book.

The history of this book began with Susan Harmon, educator and matchmaker. The manuscript itself was improved through readings by novelist Jenna Dolan and educator Sandra Wilde. Much appreciation goes to Vicki Kasabian for additional tuning of the manuscript. Thanks also go, for various reasons, to Brian Cambourne, Nancy Creecher, Pat Eastman, Linda Ellis, Shirley Ernst, Ken Goodman, Yetta Goodman, Lalia Kerr, Patricia Kimathi, Stephen Krashen, Jeff McQuillan, Leslie Paterson, Regie Routman, Dave Schultz, Tanya Sharon, Debbie Stewart, Jesse Turner, and Cheryl Weyant.

For their support, my love goes out to *tutta famiglia:* Katia, Nadia, and Walter Iannacome; Jeremy, Rom, and Terry Coles; Kim Curtis; Marianna and Miles Coles Curtis; Joci Jones; Elaine Reinhardt; and Michael and Donna Coles.

And always, for Maria, who, in Guido Cavalcanti's words, "is the pleasure in which my heart lives" (*piacer, che il mio cor sente*).

Introduction

A decade ago I could not have imagined writing this book. At that time, I praised the research on beginning reading skills; I have since come to see it as scientifically poor and its application as harmful to children who are learning to read. Although the body of research back then had been small, it appeared nonetheless to identify those literacy skills—particularly those for hearing, distinguishing, and manipulating sounds in words—that could have helped promote reading achievement or correct reading problems. I was especially attentive to the studies because I had written professional papers critical of biological explanations of reading disabilities, and this skills research seemed to support my view that reading problems could be better explained as consequences of instructional rather than biological deficiencies. The studies also appeared to offer practical applications for my work as director of a program for young adults and adults with very severe reading deficiencies.

The years that followed taught me a lesson in the risk of placing too much confidence in initial research findings. As the number of studies grew, I began to see that although the studies claimed to have found causal connections between those early reading skills and reading itself, they actually showed only correlation between the two. Just as important, the studies ignored other factors that could have caused the identified "causes." Children who learned skills that were said to be prerequisites to reading success were not learning to read any better than those not explicitly trained in those skills. Worst of all, this unsubstantial and unsubstantiated research was being called the indisputable "scientific evidence" that justified attacks on and even the dismantling of an instructional alternative, often termed *whole language*, even though the studies included virtually no examination of whole language teaching.

That alternative had arisen in response to the deficiencies of conventional reading education with its standardized, graded set of reading texts—known in the reading profession as basal readers—and instructional materials that were "organized around a hierarchy of skills and a tightly controlled vocabulary."[1] Seemingly comprehensive, the reading texts and materials encouraged excessive control of reading, language, learners, and teachers and prevented many children from learning to read. With the heralded claim of new "scientific evidence" damning whole language, the conventional education that had come under attack because of its huge failures was again being hailed as the answer to reading education, albeit with several modifications in the hierarchy of beginning reading skills. And once again, this "skills-emphasis" beginning reading instruction demanded tight control of reading, language, learners, and teachers.

The skills-emphasis view of literacy education believes that children learn best when they are first taught the basic skills of written language, especially those that take apart sounds within words, connect sounds to make words, associate sounds and letters, and identify sight words. As educational researcher Louisa Moats has stated:

> It is known that unskilled readers are unable to process efficiently and accurately the phonological building blocks of language and the units of print that represent them. Theoretical, experimental, and clinical evidence point to the necessity of helping unskilled readers and spellers acquire explicit knowledge of language structure.[2]

Attaining these skills, say proponents, should mean not merely learning them but mastering them sufficiently well to execute them rapidly. Comprehension is included marginally in this mode of beginning reading instruction, and the emphasis is on word skills. Moats and Susan Hall explain that literature stories are "selected to offer practice of phonics lesson[s]."[3] A beginning reader, the reasoning goes, must first master the skills for deciphering words and stringing them together in sentences and then rapidly apply these skills in order to understand easily the ideas in sentences, paragraphs, and stories. Educational psychologists Marilyn Adams and Maggie Bruck explain it this way:

> [S]cientific research converges on the point that the association of spellings with sounds is a fundamental step in the early stages of literacy instruction. Furthermore, reading fluency and comprehension depend not merely on knowing about these relationships but on using them, on overlearning, extending, and refining them, such that word recognition becomes fast and nearly effortless.[4]

The need to master spelling-sound word skills is especially important, skills-emphasis educators believe, because a reader has only a limited amount of memory at his or her disposal. Limited memory impedes trying to remember and associate the ideas in a sentence while at the same time trying to remember sounds associated with letters, strings of sounds, words already identified, and similar small but essential parts of a sentence. These educators believe that beginning reading instruction that emphasizes skills and de-emphasizes the comprehension of meaning thereby enables a beginning reader to use memory efficiently.

As I have already said, this step-by-step, tightly controlled, direct, explicit, and systematic teaching of a "predetermined logical sequence" of beginning reading skills is believed by its proponents to be not merely a successful method but one superior to "whole language," the teaching approach identified as its primary adversary.[5] As its name implies, whole language engages beginning readers in the entirety of written language. It emphasizes comprehending the meaning *in* written language and connecting the meaning *of* written language to the lives of readers.

Whole language maintains that children's motivation for learning written language is similar to that which impelled their learning of oral language: the desire to make meaning in order to participate and communicate within a community of language users. Just as their making of and communicating with oral meaning was the overarching orchestration that promoted their pronunciation of words, use of words to identify multiple objects, stringing words into sentences, syntax, and vocabulary development, and so forth, making of and communicating with *written* meaning has similar effects. For example, when children pretend to write, use a single letter for a word, write "I love you," identify a word on a page, memorize portions or all of a story that has been read and reread to them, etc., they are learning and *are being helped to learn* numerous facets of written language, such as sounds in words, syllabication, sound-symbol relationships, correct spelling, and common letter-sound clusters (e.g., *ing, at*) that end words. For these reasons, as language arts resource teacher Regie Routman has emphasized, "inquiry and language in authentic use [is] at the heart" of the whole language curriculum.

> Meaning and knowledge are constructed from the learner's experiences. Comprehension is always the objective. Skills and isolated facts are not relevant unless they take on a personal meaning. Whole language teachers believe that children learn best when curriculum is personally meaningful and relevant to their lives.[6]

Addressing misconceptions of whole language, such as the belief that whole language teachers simply create a print-rich environment and then let children intuitively learn to read, Routman has stressed that whole language

- teaches the "basics," but in meaningful literacy contexts;
- provides explicit instruction when students' needs and interests require it;
- provides rigorous teaching with high expectations; and
- is greatly concerned with learning outcomes.[7]

Skills-emphasis and whole language teaching also have different conceptions of how children should participate in their literacy education, with whole language putting greater emphasis on social relationships, student participation, and learning in a community. Susan Church, superintendent of educational services in Halifax, Nova Scotia, has described how "as a teacher," she has tried

> to create a learning community in which learners have many opportunities to interact, to share their diverse perspectives, and to learn from each other. I work to make the learning community inclusive by inviting the participation of all: students, teachers, administrators, parents, and other adults. Within this social learning environment, there is ongoing negotiation of power and control. Teachers and learners work to develop social relationships that reflect democratic principles.[8]

Whole language proponents consider these concerns to be not simply *add-ons* to literacy learning, but part of the *whole* social context that fosters children's ongoing reading and writing efforts and progress. Children's active participation in a learning community is inextricably linked to their active, motivated, and meaningful literacy learning. Literacy learning contributes to participation in the learning community and vice versa.

The instructional approach a teacher or school system chooses has always been based on a number of considerations, among which are published research, educational philosophies, published anecdotes, individual and school experiences, teacher education courses, test outcomes, child development values, political pressures, school budgets, and professional organization endorsements. The mix of these and other influences on decision making has led, for better and worse, to beginning literacy education that has ranged from rigid, authoritarian, and mindless to flexible, democratic, and creative. In the conflicts over how to teach reading and writing, there has been disagreement over which elements in the mix should count more than others and which should not count at all. Generally speaking, a pluralism of considerations has been accepted as part of the decision-making process as long as reading education does not stray too far from the "tried-and-true" conventional, preplanned reading curriculum administered by teachers and ingested by students. When it does, champions of the conventional curriculum usually narrow the standards for decision making, with achievement test scores leading the backlash. Test results that seem to document plunging levels of reading achievement alarm policy makers and the public, although later studies might show that the scores had not lowered or, if they had, could not be attributed to reading reforms. By the time these corrections appear, however, the backlash has already succeeded. The series of attacks on Open Classroom reforms of the 1960s is one example of false claims about lower reading achievement; attacks on whole language reforms in California during the 1980s and 1990s are instances of both false claims about lowered reading achievement and false explanations of what accounted for reading test results.[9]

Accusations of lowered reading test results are one-half of the arsenal used by supporters of conventional reading education, who also claim that their views are not mere opinion but are based on research that leaves no doubt about the need to scrap the newest reform, whole language, and to institute skills-emphasis teaching.

The influence of these claims has been far-reaching and successful. Between 1990 and 1997, legislation was introduced in twenty-six states encouraging or requiring the direct, explicit, and systematic use of phonics and similar word skills in beginning reading instruction. With each passing year, the number of state legislatures considering such bills—several of which have "punitive provisions" for noncompliance—has increased. As school law specialist Francis Paterson documents, from the end of 1994 through 1997, the number of state legislatures in which such bills have been introduced increased from eight to fourteen.[10]

A 1997 education bill in California (AB 1086) included funds for professional development programs for teachers of reading that had to be conducted by "approved providers" who met criteria established by the state Board of Education. Educators with extensive publishing records and teacher-training backgrounds but affiliated with whole language were uniformly rejected as providers, no matter how they proposed teaching skills. Teaching skills as part of a comprehensive (whole) written language curriculum was not acceptable. The reason for this rejection was apparent in the bill's requirements: professional development had to include training in the direct, systematic teaching of phonemic awareness, phonics, and decoding and the diagnosis of students' competence in these skills. Only educators who demonstrated conformity with the requirements became eligible to receive state money.[11]

This training requirement was only a small part of the policy changes in California. At the local level, for example, the superintendent of the Los Angeles schools ordered "that phonics be made a mandatory part" of reading instruction, but not a "part" of other reading activities. "Phonics" meant phonics lessons that would "stand alone as a teaching tool."[12]

The 1999 national conference of the International Reading Association, held in San Diego, included panel presentations objecting to the restrictive state literacy policies, and many whole language advocates wore T-shirts reading "Banned in California." In response, Marion Joseph, a member of the state Board of Education and "largely credited with setting California on the phonics path," no doubt expressed the sentiment of many of the state's policy makers when she called the International Reading Association the "heart and soul of the whole language movement" and recommended: "We think we've had enough advice from them. Why don't they go someplace else?"[13]

That "someplace else" probably would not have been Washington, D.C., where skills-emphasis teaching was the focus of research funded by the National Institute of Child Health and Human Development (NICHD). Typical of this teaching was a classroom in which a teacher "extolled the long 'e' in the word 'cheek.'" The exuberant response of students was echoed in other classes, where students could "be heard chanting letter sounds, reading in unison and practicing rhyming and other exercises."[14]

Appraising the conflict between whole language educators and those critical of it, a *Baltimore Sun* education reporter wrote,

> the whole language movement is clearly at a disadvantage. The pendulum is swinging toward phonics, and phonics proponents have the weight of science on their side. Much of the recent research on reading has been conducted not by educators, but by scientists in the employ of the [NICHD division of the] National Institutes of Health.[15]

In Texas, a beginning reading program called Open Court, which emphasizes phonemic awareness (the awareness of sounds within words) and related skills, was reported to be extraordinarily more successful than other instructional approaches, especially whole language, in teaching poor children. "You can take [this] classroom program and get all but 4.5 percent up to the national average—that's astounding," commented Barbara Foorman, the leading researcher of an NICHD-supported study that made the comparison.[16]

Reports of this kind of success helped convince the Baltimore school board to mandate the use of Open Court for "all children in kindergarten through second grade."[17] In Brooklyn, New York, Open Court's similar success with poor children was praised by Diane Ravitch, a prominent educator and former U.S. assistant secretary for educational research in the George Bush administration. What was the instructional "secret"? asked Ravitch. "No secret," she concluded, just the use of "time-tested instructional methods in reading":

> No pedagogical fads. No invented spelling, no whole-language reading, no guessing at words in context. Every teacher teaches intensive phonics, using the Open Court readers. Most children are reading in kindergarten. In every classroom children sound out syllables and words, and their joy in learning is apparent.[18]

In October 1998, the Senate passed the Reading Excellence Act (H.R. 2514). Although many of its aims are commendable—it provided grants to states for inservice training of teachers, after-school tutoring in schools with high numbers of poor children, and family literacy programs—its major potential impact on literacy education was in its explicit definitions of reading, reading instruction, and "reliable" research, all of which emphasize teaching skills and might find their way into other reading legislation and teacher education. At the forefront of the definition of beginning reading competence were "the skills and knowledge to understand how phonemes, or speech sounds, are connected to print" and "the ability to decode unfamiliar words." Instructional practices were to be derived from "scientifically based reading research," a term appearing twenty-nine times in the text of the act. At first glance, the term might seem reasonable, but as whole language educator Ken Goodman observed, the term was code for a particular paradigm of research and views of reading, one that dismissed whole language research as unscientific but regarded as scientific the body of studies that emphasized the need for early, direct, systematic, and explicit instruction of skills.[19] In the words of Robert Sweet Jr., founder of the National Right to Read Foundation, an organization that does "battle to bring phonics back to our schools," and a congressional staff member who helped draft the bill, the act was "a breakthrough for reading teacher training."[20]

The words *science* and *scientific,* used to bolster these policy and legislative efforts, are composed of several claims. One is that scientific research has identified the chief cause of reading success and failure. Another is that scientific research has made great and usable strides in identifying the best method for teaching reading. A third says that if this method were applied to classrooms, it would ensure that most children would learn to read.

"Scientific" reading research seems to have acquired a boundless authority and influence. Around the nation, school systems have been purchasing reading programs purportedly validated by scientific research. Typical of the belief that science was now shaping reading education was a statement by Duane Alexander, director of the NICHD. "Research supported [by the institute]," he said, "is altering the [reading] field and offering teachers a scientific basis for teaching reading."[21]

Similarly, G. Reid Lyon, chief of the division of the Child Development and Behavior Branch of the NICHD that has funded this research, noted that the "NICHD reading research program is rooted in scientific tradition and the scientific method" and has "nearly four decades of [this] scientific research" on "how children learn to read." Despite these accomplishments and the hope that scientific research would inform "beginning reading instruction," he lamented, that has "not always [been] so." The research information was available, Lyon declared, but teachers and administrators had difficulty setting aside scientifically unsubstantiated "assumptions that are not working" and lacked the "trust" that scientific research could "inform their teaching."[22] I have quoted these two leading members of the NICHD because that organization has been in the forefront of claims about prodigious scientific findings in beginning reading education that have been used to justify major policy and legislative changes.

Invoking science for solutions to literacy problems has a strong appeal partly because important scientific contributions in this century have helped us understand how people read and how reading should be taught. Compared with other avenues for obtaining knowledge, science is also relatively more systematic, formal, and objective. On the other hand, there have been and are good reasons for skepticism about scientific explanations and solutions. From IQ testing to tobacco research, a long line of reports about scientific "truths" have later been shown to be pseudoscientific, sometimes based on consciously manipulated—and even invented—data aimed at "documenting" a predetermined outcome.[23] For some critics, these false claims have justified a total rejection of science—a rejection of notions of objectivity and truth—and an exaltation of alternative ways of knowing.[24]

I do not share this view. The subtitle of this book, *The Bad Science That Hurts Children*, uses the term *bad* to distinguish between research done well or poorly, and my use of the term implicitly carries a belief in the value of science.

This book is primarily about a body of research on reading that I consider "bad." The studies have the appearance of valid empiricism. Their experimental and control groups and subjects are selected according to definable characteristics, such as whether they can hear sounds in words, associate alphabet sounds and letters, or read phonetic "nonsense" words like *baf* or *gib*. Research questions are carefully defined, and instructional methods and reading tests are employed to help answer the questions. Data are statistically analyzed and discussed in detail. Yet, I will argue in the chapters ahead that a close look at the skills-emphasis research reveals that below a veneer of adherence to scientific standards is an extensive pattern of faulty research designs, data, logic, and interpretations that offers little support for the strong conclusions about the "scientific" findings that have been proclaimed.

If the research were simply cloistered within professional journals and conferences—if it were solely "pure" research seeking to determine causal influences on learning to read—it could be considered work poorly done but without injurious consequences. Unfortunately, not only has it been used to justify policy and legislation that narrow alternatives for teachers and other school personnel but it has also been harmful because it falsely holds out the promise of a simple, "magic bullet" solution to the literacy failure of millions of children, especially those who are poor, while at the same time discouraging social policy attention to forces both in and out of schools that influence literacy outcomes. The research has also defined literacy success in thin, rigid terms that ignore countless matters about the purposes of education.

The aim of this book is to discuss this body of research. Included in this research are studies comparing skills-emphasis and whole language teaching, but for several reasons I will not extend the discussion to research by proponents of whole language. First, whether whole language is effective is, as I have said, a question running throughout this skills-emphasis research. Therefore, my discussion of whole language will be centered on whether this research does, in fact, provide a scientific repudiation of whole language. Arguing beyond this—that is, for or against the merits of whole language instruction and research—would require another book.[25]

Second, asking which beginning reading instruction is more effective is the wrong question. Although "What is the best way to teach reading?" is a vital question, it is relatively limited compared with another question: "What needs to be done to ensure that children learn to read?" This second question encompasses the first, but unlike the first—which is usually a meaningless "horse race" question—it also includes the array of influences both inside and outside the classroom that contribute to literacy success and failure. "What is the best way to teach reading?" also requires addressing the question "What kind of thinking, feeling, and acting should literacy education encourage?" This question is implicit in and inseparable from all reading instruction and all education and also needs to be addressed when identifying and appraising the respective merits of instruction.[26]

Beyond the recent instructional, policy, and legislative history I have outlined in this introduction, I also will not delve into the practical consequences of this research. Others have discussed many of these consequences,[27] but there has not yet been a full, critical examination of the research that has underpinned them. What I hope to achieve by the end of this book is an appraisal that readers can use when confronting the practical consequences in their schools; parent associations; policy meetings at the community, state, or federal level; education courses; teacher professional development programs; or the media.

The book is structured around the primary claims of skills-emphasis research that have been used to influence policy and legislation, and it uses a simple method that first identifies a claim and then examines the evidence for the claim. Chief among these claims are the following:

- Phonemic awareness is the chief causal influence in learning to read.
- Skills-training programs facilitate learning to read and remediate reading problems.
- Research has demonstrated the superiority of skills-emphasis over whole language instruction.
- The effectiveness of a widely acclaimed skills-emphasis reading program has been demonstrated in published research.
- A brain "glitch" associated with phonemic awareness is responsible for the reading problems of many children.
- Phonemic awareness problems can be traced to genetic causes.

Offering a readable, comprehensive review of the skills-emphasis research is, frankly, a daunting task because of the many studies constituting this corpus of work and the need to discuss them in sufficient but not excessive detail. Having gone through these studies end to end, I have chosen to examine only those that prominent skills-emphasis researchers themselves have cited as principal works. Like these researchers, I believe that the works they draw upon adequately represent similar studies less frequently cited. I have also tried to pare away extraneous details and focus on the substance of the studies. And I have tried to translate professional jargon into plain English.

I have dedicated this book to two dear friends and exemplary educators, Milton and Bernice Schwebel. In 1968, Milt wrote *Who Can Be Educated?*, a book arguing that a first-class education for all children was a goal the United States had yet to achieve.[28] While reviewing the historical conflicts between those who worked for this goal and others who opposed it, he remarked, "How different American education might have been if at one of its key points of choice the nation had taken an alternative path."[29]

Thirty years later, this observation remains current and especially germane to the issues in this book. I hope to show there is every reason to reject the path of skills-emphasis teaching ostensibly illuminated by new scientific light and return to the juncture where we can change directions. Although the purpose of the book is not to outline an alternative path, I hope to demonstrate the need for educators to adopt the initial charge in the Hippocratic oath: like physicians, we must first do no harm. If we do not reject the misleading "scientifically based" literacy research as a guide for policy and legislation, the alternative path surely will come too late for the countless and inevitable casualties of the education it favors.

CLAIM

Phonemic awareness (hearing, distinguishing, and manipulating the sounds in words) is the chief causal factor in early reading achievement and the "core deficit" in reading problems.

WHAT THE RESEARCH ACTUALLY SHOWS

- ☐ "Skilled readers" do better than "less-skilled" readers only on phonemic awareness and related skills tests, but the studies show only correlations, not causation. They do not show *how* skills and reading achievement are correlated or if some other influence—such as the classroom instruction itself or preschool literacy experience—is actually responsible for the correlation.
- ☐ The studies provide information about associations between phonemic awareness and reading, but information is not itself explanation.
- ☐ Studies have shown that training in narrow skills, such as phonemic awareness, helps children do better on tests of these and related skills but does not improve reading comprehension of sentences or stories, or make a difference in later reading achievement.
- ☐ The large quantity and repetitious citations of research papers on skills-teaching and reading evade the problem of the low quality of the studies.

1

Erecting the "Strong Consensus"

In recent years, the argument driving the skills-first research has had two parts, one positive, the other negative. The positive side claims that beginning readers need direct, explicit instruction in written language skills to get a fast start in reading. The negative argument dismisses whole language as a productive teaching approach. In some ways this argument is a new form of a very old contention—going back at least two centuries in Europe and the United States—that in beginning reading, it is better to emphasize skills rather than meaning. We can trace this back to the ABC approach used in Germany in the late eighteenth century, which began with the alphabet, continued through syllables, words, and sentences, and moved eventually to books; the phonics method prevalent in reading textbooks through the nineteenth century; and the twentieth-century claims of neurologist Samuel Orton and his followers that phonics is the answer to preventing and overcoming reading disabilities.[1]

The skills-first argument gained strength in the 1950s with the publication of *Why Johnny Can't Read*, Rudolf Flesch's polemical attack on the dominant teaching method, variously called whole word, look-and-say, or sight word teaching. Flesch called for the resurrection of phonics-first instruction, maintaining that before the appearance of "word learning" around 1925, there had "never been a [reading] problem anywhere in the world."[2] Although the book was a best-seller, it failed to bring about the changes Flesch advocated, leading him to write *Why Johnny Still Can't Read* in 1981, described by the publisher as an "incendiary sequel."[3]

The skills-first drama acquired a more academic cast in Jeanne Chall's 1967 book *Learning to Read: The Great Debate*. Published at a time of widespread educational reforms and experimentation, including approaches in beginning reading that stressed engaging children in meaningful written language activities, Chall's book made the case for a tightly controlled beginning reading instruction. Chall, a professor of education at Harvard University, reviewed fifty years of research on the "meaning-emphasis method" ("believes that children should, and do, learn to read best when meaning is emphasized from the start") versus the "code-emphasis method" ("believes that the initial stage of reading instruction should emphasize teaching children to master a code—the alphabetic code"). She concluded that the latter produced superior results.[4]

Code-emphasis instruction got another boost in *Becoming a Nation of Readers*, a 1985 report by the Commission on Reading, of which Jeanne Chall was a member. The report referred to Chall's "now-classic book" and concluded that the issue was no longer "whether children should be taught phonics. The issues now are specific ones of just how it should be done."[5] William Bennett, secretary of education under Ronald Reagan, reiterated the report's recommendations in two of his own books on elementary education.[6]

The research I will discuss is a continuation of this legacy lauding skills, although is not a simple reprise of arguments for phonics and even appears to be critical of earlier recommendations for phonics-first teaching. Now we supposedly have breakthrough research precisely identifying the written language skills that promote beginning reading. For all its newness and attempt to distance itself from the past, however, a close examination of this research reveals that it has a fairly seamless connection to its predecessors.

Since the studies of the last ten years are most often cited as justification for a skills emphasis in policy and legislation on beginning reading, most of this book will concentrate on that research. However, both to understand this research fully and to appraise the foundation upon which policy and legislation rest, we need to look back at work done in the previous decade from which all of the current work draws heavily.

The "Core Deficit" in Learning to Read

The research used on behalf of what is claimed to be the need for a skills emphasis has been built largely around a skill called *phonemic awareness* (or *phonological awareness*), a skill said to be a necessary forerunner of phonics skills (connecting sounds and symbols). The terms *phonological awareness* and *phonemic awareness* refer to the knowledge that phonemes (the smallest units of speech sounds) are separable and can be manipulated mentally and orally, as when blending or separating phonemes in order to identify words. A blending task might ask someone to blend phonemes into a word and say it (/r/, /a/, /t/ = rat). A task showing that a youngster can segment phonemes could ask which sounds are heard in a word (rat = /r/a/t/). A task requiring the deletion of phonemes might ask what word would remain if a phoneme were deleted (remove /r/ from rat).

Phonological awareness is considered not only important in learning to read but a key—if not *the* key—causal influence in the process. This view cannot be emphasized too strongly at the beginning of our discussion because virtually all the skills-emphasis research is aimed at proving this point. It is the principal view running through all research on and advocacy for a skills-first emphasis.

For example, Reid Lyon, chief of the division of the National Institute of Child Health and Human Development (NICHD) that has funded much of the research in question, summarized the "major findings" of NICHD research in this way:

> Deficits in phonological awareness reflect the core deficit in dyslexia. . . . The best predictor of reading ability from kindergarten and first-grade performance is phoneme segmentation ability . . . There is strong evidence for a genetic basis for reading disabilities, with deficits in phonological awareness reflecting the greatest degree of heritability.[7]

Similarly, Sally Shaywitz, a reading researcher and a leading recipient of NICHD funding, stated: "Evidence from a number of lines of investigation has now converged to identify and isolate a component within the language system, phonological processing, as the specific cognitive deficit responsible for reading disability."[8]

And Keith Stanovich, a prominent reading researcher and theoretician, who will be discussed at length in this chapter, offered this summation in 1994: "In the last 10 years, researchers have come to a strong consensus about the cognitive processes that best predict reading progress in the earliest stages. These cognitive processes have been called phonological awareness."[9]

Antecedents to Today's Research

During the 1980s, running through virtually all articles and research publications promoting skills-emphasis instruction is the work of Keith Stanovich. In 1995 the International Reading Association, having identified Stanovich as a "distinguished educator," elected him to the association's Hall of Fame. Stanovich is a prolific writer whose publications flow through the skills-emphasis literature, and, arguably, no one has had more influence on this literature's theory, research, and conclusions over the last two decades. Stanovich's writings, therefore, provide the opportunity to identify important skills-emphasis research during these decades.

Finding Causal Connections

We will begin our discussion of the research on causal connections between phonological awareness and reading by looking at a 1984 study done by Stanovich and his colleagues.[10] In May, kindergartners from middle-class families were given a number of phonological tasks, and their reading ability was assessed during the following May. As we shall see, this is a common research method in these studies: to test for skills at one point, give reading tests at another, and correlate the results of both.

The follow-up found that those students who had become "skilled readers" had done significantly better on most of the phonological tasks than had the "less-skilled" readers, leading the researchers to conclude that the phonological tasks were "quite impressive predictors of first-grade reading ability." Although they cautioned that "the relationship between reading ability and phonological awareness seems to be characterized by reciprocal causation," whatever might have been assessed as reciprocal vanished with their proposal that "the causal connection at the earliest stages of reading acquisition is probably most strong from phonological awareness to increased reading acquisition."[11]

The study itself offered no grounds for this speculation about causation because it provided only correlational information. Furthermore, although one part of early reading abilities was isolated—that is, phonological awareness—we know nothing about the youngsters' other written language abilities. How well could they read? What words did they know? How might these other abilities have been connected to later reading achievement? More important, we have no information about the experiences that might have produced the kindergartners' various phonological abilities. Nor do we know anything about the education of the children when they were in first grade. For example, were they tracked in school and did this tracking reinforce any initial differences?

We have here our first insight into "bad" science, a failure to distinguish between information and explanation. The study does offer information about an association between phonological awareness and reading but then makes the unwarranted leap of treating correlation as causation. Although considerable information is lacking even to understand the meaning of the correlation, the limited data become transformed into meaningful conclusions, resting on qualifiers such as *probably.*

The "Causal Connection"

Stanovich and his colleagues draw not only on their own study in proposing that "the causal connection" runs from "phonological aware-ness to increased reading acquisition"[12] but also cite two others. This is a legitimate practice in all scholarly work, of course, provided that the studies cited include evidence to support the claims about them.

One publication cited is by psychologists Rebecca Treiman and Jonathan Baron, who trained preschool and kindergarten prereaders in phonological awareness in two experiments. In the beginning phase of the first experiment, lasting four days, a group of children learned to segment four spoken syllables into their initial consonants and remain-ing portions—for example, the children learned to respond to *hem* as *h* and *em*). A control group was exposed to four different syllables, but rather than segmenting them, the children just repeated them aloud. Both groups were then taught to do a reading task in which they learned to read "items that corresponded to the spoken syllables with which they had worked in the first place" and other "items" that did not correspond to the syllables they had learned. The trained group made fewer mistakes in learning the words related to the sound patterns they had practiced in training.[13]

A second experiment provided training in segmentation and blending of words, and again the trained children made fewer mistakes learning words related to the sounds in which they had been trained.

From these brief experiments, Treiman and Baron concluded "that phonemic-analysis training can promote reading skill." Strictly speaking, of course, the conclusion could be said to be true, but *read-ing skill* is not the same as *reading.* That is, there is no evidence that this training has any positive effect on full reading tasks such as reading and comprehending sentences, paragraphs, and stories, and there is no rea-son to assume that studies of few days' durations can reveal much about reading outcomes over time.[14] Citing the study, as Stanovich and his colleagues do, as support for the claim that "the causal connection at the earliest stages of reading acquisition is probably most strong from phonological awareness to increased reading acquisition" is more than a stretch.[15]

Another research paper Stanovich cites was written by British psychologists Lynette Bradley and Peter Bryant.[16] They measured the ability of four- and five-year-old nonreaders to categorize sounds by asking them to detect the odd word among the ones that matched in sound (e.g., *bud, bun, bus, rug*). High correlations were found between the initial sound-categorization scores and reading and spelling test scores three years later.

Another phase of this study selected sixty-five children among those who scored lowest in sound categorization. These children were divided into four groups, two of which received training in sound categorization—for example, learning which words shared beginning, middle, and ending sounds. One of these two groups used plastic letters to help learn the common sounds. The third group learned how to classify the sounds by categories—for example, *hen* and *bat* are animals. The fourth group received no training. At the end of the training period, the two groups that received sound-categorization training had statistically superior scores in reading and spelling, with the second group (those that used plastic letters) scoring better than the first.

The study shows that specific training in phonological awareness *and* sound-symbol relationships can lead children to earn better reading and spelling scores than if children do not receive this training. Conclusions beyond this are limited because there is no meaningful comparison group that would provide an insight into alternative approaches to reading success. The control groups received no alternative written language education; no information was provided about the literacy education the children received in the classroom; there was no demonstration of the need to improve reading this particular way rather than another way. Therefore, the study does not lend support to Stanovich's interpretation that phonological awareness is the "most strong" causal influence in learning to read. Stanovich's phrase "most strong" implies that there was an array of comparisons with other kinds of written language education, an implication not justified by this study.

"Decoding Speed" and Comprehension

In another 1984 study, Stanovich and his colleagues concluded that "decoding speed"—the speed at which a reader can name words and pseudowords—had a major positive influence on reading comprehension. The researchers interpreted this connection to mean that the better a student is at connecting sounds with symbols or symbol units— the "phonological code"—the faster the student will be able to identify and comprehend words.[17] Decoding speed is considered by these researchers as the foundation for comprehending written material because, they hypothesize, since a beginning reader has only a limited amount of memory, rapidly decoding and identifying words allows him or her to devote more memory to comprehension. Anyone who has worked with beginning readers is familiar with the problem this interpretation seems to address: a reader who has considerable difficulty identifying written words is likely to be impaired when trying to string those words together into a meaningful sentence.

There is sense in this interpretation: the more words a reader knows when reading a sentence or story, the more the reader will be able to concentrate on comprehending what is read. What does not follow—but which slips into Stanovich's formulation—is that decoding is the necessary antecedent to word recognition. That is, if we were to change the term *decoding speed* to *word-recognition speed,* we would change the conception of how a reader learns to read words rapidly from a primary dependency on decoding to one contingent on other written language information.

Anyone who has worked with beginning readers also knows that recognizing and reading rapidly a sufficient number of words in a sentence in order to comprehend the sentence does not require an extensive focus on decoding. Sentence and story comprehension are achievable by using books within a reader's reading ability, in which most of the words are familiar to the reader but a small number of unknown words can nevertheless be identified by drawing upon the meaning already understood in the sentence, the syntax of the sentence, *and* decoding skills. As for the question of how words are learned in the first place, a variety of written language information can be incorporated, with decoding only one of these tools. In addition, the use of writing in literacy development is a key activity that contributes to learning words, becoming increasingly familiar with them, and learning to read them rapidly.

How does this issue of the effect of alternative instruction on rapid word recognition bear upon this study by Stanovich and colleagues? We have no way of knowing. Their report provides no information about how the first, third, and fifth graders in the study were instructed, and therefore, we have no information about what produced the decoding speed and comprehension outcomes and their correlations. Again, correlation does not demonstrate causation. It *might* be true that phonological awareness is causally related to decoding skills, which in turn influence how much children are able to practice reading, which in turn influences the speed at which words are recognized, which in turn influences the ability to read for meaning, which in turn influences comprehension achievement. This might be a logical model, but the data in this study makes it no more than speculative.

Implicating Phonemic Analysis

To support their view that "phonological awareness is probably causally related to the early acquisition of decoding skills,"[18] Stanovich and his colleagues cite additional studies. One of these was by reading educator Barbara Fox and psychologist Donald Routh, who used the common method of testing youngsters in phonemic analysis and appraising its association with reading achievement. In this study, first graders were tested at the end of the school year in their ability to segment spoken syllables into phonemes and were then divided according to their reading ability: average readers, children with mild reading difficulties, and those with a severe reading disability. The test scores of the last group were "markedly lower than those of other groups," which, for the researchers, "strongly implicate[d] the process of phoneme analysis in the initial stages of a child's learning to read."[19]

Contrary to this conclusion, and in keeping with the studies discussed above, there is little here to be concluded about phonemic awareness because we know nothing about the instruction used, except that it employed a basal reading program. To what extent was the program implicated in the divergence in reading achievement? We do not know. To what extent did the program stress and require phonemic skills and thereby impair children who might have learned better through another approach? We do not know. To what extent did the program encourage a one-size-fits-all approach that did not fit all the children? We do not know. To what extent was the basal reading program the key causal influence? We do not know. What other kinds of written language experience did the groups have prior to attending school that might have influenced reading outcomes? We do not know. In other words, this is one more study in which we learn little about the relationship between phonemic skills and reading and what it means to say that the relationship is causal.

In a follow-up study using the same group of average readers, now in the fourth grade, and the severely disabled readers, who after being left back a year were now only in third grade, the connection between phonemic skills and reading achievement was again examined. Interestingly, the two groups had a number of similar scores: they "did not differ" on the number of phonetic words they knew by sight, the percentage of phonetic sight vocabulary they spelled correctly, the number of nonphonetic words they knew by sight, the percentage of nonphonetic vocabulary they spelled correctly, or the percentage of unknown phonetic words they spelled correctly. The two groups did differ significantly on their spelling errors, with the reading-disabled group exhibiting many phonics errors ("dysphonetic spelling" patterns).[20]

These spelling errors constituted the key finding for the researchers, who apparently had no interest in pursuing the meaning of the comparable scores of both groups. Surely the similar scores might have raised the hypothesis that because the children had continued to improve their phonemic skills, perhaps other problems contributed to their reading problems.

Again—and in keeping with the other studies we have discussed—these two studies offer little to support Stanovich's claim that "phonological awareness is probably causally related to the early acquisition of decoding skills."

"The Linkage Is Causal"

To bolster the claim, Stanovich also cites a study by educational researcher Charles Perfetti and his colleagues. (Stanovich cites a conference paper, here I discuss a published version of the study.) The investigators posed a research hypothesis that left open the precise relationships of phonemic knowledge and reading: the "essential question is whether phonemic knowledge allows reading or whether reading allows phonemic knowledge."[21]

The study used three groups of first graders. The first, a "direct code group," was "taught reading by a systematic direct code instruction program," that is, a phonics program that emphasized letter-sound correspondences and blending. The two other groups were taught with a basal reader series—a standardized, graded set of reading textbooks and materials organized around a hierarchy of skills and vocabulary—but "did not receive direct phonics instruction."[22] One of the basal reader groups (the "readiness" group) began first grade with a reading readiness workbook—a book containing exercises believed to be prerequisites for learning to read, such as naming and distinguishing colors and shapes, memory exercises, and identifying words that have the same beginning or ending sound—because the teachers did not consider them ready to begin work in the basal reader. The other group had abilities sufficient for beginning with a basal reader.

From the test results, the researchers proposed that "phonemic knowledge and learning to read develop in mutual support" and that even though some rudimentary phonemic skills "may be necessary for significant progress in reading," it is "reading itself that enables the child to be able to analyze words and to manipulate their speech segments."[23]

The study supplied some information on the racial and social class differences among the groups, some of which was striking. The readiness group was 50 percent or more black children, while the basal reader group was predominantly white. Some figures that hint at the influences of these differences are the percentile levels on the reading readiness test and their relationship to children's placement in the school curriculum. The percentile levels were higher for the basal reading group (47–97) than for the reading readiness group (22–90), although the upper range for both groups overlapped. One can only wonder, then, why a child with a percentile score of 90 was put in the reading readiness group—again, the majority of whom were black—while another child with a score of 47 was placed in the advanced basal reader group—the majority of whom were white. The implication of this question for exploring deeper causal influences on learning to read in first grade evoked no discussion by the investigators.

Nor was there any discussion on the influence that instruction could have had in creating the reading-achievement differences. The readiness group began reading instruction primarily with a workbook program. Did the researchers believe this was the best approach for teaching children who had less "reading readiness" than their classmates? Did instruction in "readiness" exercises rather than in actual reading of easy-to-read children's books have any bearing on the relationship between reading and skills? Does the reading approach matter? The discussion section in the study fails to address these kinds of questions. Questions about instructional approach bring up a critical issue for current discussions of this body of research: neither this nor the previous studies discussed made any use of a whole language approach.

Finally, we return to the question of citation evidence for conclusions about the causal influence of phonemic awareness. The investigators emphasize "mutual support" and also offer a caveat about drawing conclusions about causation: "the question of whether phonemic knowledge enables reading or reading enables phonemic knowledge is difficult, because the data are correlational."[24] Despite these remarks, Stanovich cited the study in a paper to support the claim that "the linkage from phonological processing ability to reading skill is a causal one."[25]

What Is the Meaning of "Linked"?

A 1973 study by educational researcher Robert Calfee and colleagues looked at the development of phonological skills from kindergarten through twelfth grade and their relationship to reading and spelling achievement.[26] Stanovich and his colleagues cite this as part of "much recent research [that] has linked phonological awareness to early success in reading acquisition."[27] The researchers found that "relatively simple phonological skills are significantly and substantially related to reading and spelling performance through high school." However, the researchers also noted that "this was a correlational study." [28] Hence, any conclusions about causation are purely speculation. As in other research, there was no exploration of the classroom teaching that contributed to phonological awareness and reading achievement.

The Matthew Effects

In 1986, Stanovich wrote a paper that has become highly regarded among many literacy educators; in publications on the importance of phonemic awareness and phonics, it is rare not to find it cited.[29] The paper introduced *Matthew effects,* a term taken from a biblical passage that describes the rich-get-richer-and-the-poor-get-poorer phenomenon. The paper applied the phenomenon to reading by drawing the analogy that differences in early reading success lead to later huge differences in literacy and academic achievement. Central in these Matthew effects, Stanovich argued, were differences in the ease with which children broke the spelling-sound code: the more rapidly they did so, the more extensively they would eventually be able to read and the more other academic achievements would accrue. Those who had more difficulty cracking the code would have more limited reading experiences and ultimately less academic success.

In this formulation, Stanovich reiterated the view of earlier papers: the early, rapid acquisition of skills is the key for creating a large number of "rich" readers. The "evidence is mounting," he stated, "that the primary specific mechanism that enables early reading success is phonological awareness" because "phonological awareness stands out as the most potent predictor" of reading acquisition.[30] To support this, he cited several publications, two of which were his 1984 papers that I discussed above.[31] Another study cited was by reading researcher David Share and his colleagues.

Are "Predictive Correlations" Causes?

Share and his colleagues found that the strongest predictors of the reading achievement of first graders were their test scores, obtained shortly after they began kindergarten, on phoneme segmentation, letter names, finger localization (a child whose vision is blocked identifies which of her or his fingers an adult has touched), and letter copying. Does this predictive strength mean that kindergartners need to learn these abilities in order to get off to a fast, secure start in reading? For knowing letter names, the researchers' answer is "No." They point out that although "knowledge of letter names has been traditionally considered the single best predictor of reading achievement . . . there appears to be no evidence that letter-name knowledge facilitates reading acquisition."[32] We would assume, therefore, that letter-name knowledge represents experience and accomplishments that are part of and contribute to literacy attainment; the knowledge is a "marker" of these experiences and accomplishments.

The same could certainly be said for finger localization, the third-strongest-ranked predictor of first-grade reading achievement. The test for this ability consisted of a child's hand being hidden from the child's view while a tester touched one or more fingers and then asked the child which ones were touched. Despite its correlation with future reading achievement—despite the fact that, according to Share and his colleagues, it is a predictor—the skill itself could not be considered causal to learning to read, and no educator would suggest finger-localization training as a beginning reading method. We have in these predictors "products" related to reading achievement, but we have no information on the learning processes through which these products were obtained and the extent to which these products might be markers of other experiences and teaching more closely related to reading attainment.

Finally, there is the very serious question of why preschool abilities should preordain future reading achievement. Are deficiencies in these abilities something the children could not overcome regardless of teaching approaches used? Did the seeming preordination represent other characteristics that actually influenced reading outcomes? Were the instructional methods, more than the phonemic abilities, the determinants of reading achievement? Although the researchers did minimal analysis of the instructional methods and provided only the scantest discussion of instructional methods that seemed to be relatively homogeneous and geared little toward individual differences in children's learning, they concluded that the methods appeared to be of a "minor influence."[33]

Regardless of their interpretations of the data, the investigators themselves caution, "these predictive correlations do not provide direct support for causal relationships. Only experimental studies can establish these."[34] In short, the study provides little explanation of the meaning of the "predictors."

"Not Proof," But . . .

In his "Matthew Effects" paper, Stanovich does acknowledge that the aforementioned study and others he cites offer only correlational findings, "not proof that variation in awareness is causally connected to differences in the ease of initial reading acquisition. Proving causation requires much stronger evidence, and this evidence is much less plentiful than the purely correlational data." Despite this caveat, however, he again restates the primary assertion: "a growing body of data does exist indicating that variation in phonological awareness is causally related to the early development of reading skill."[35]

To his credit, he acknowledges that several studies support the view that "reading acquisition itself facilitates phonological awareness, so that the situation appears to be one of reciprocal causation," yet then dismisses this, going on to say—for reasons he does not explain—that "reciprocal causation" seems to have little place in the model of learning to read that he proposes. The "essential properties" of this model, he asserts, are "dependent only on the fact that a causal link running from phonological awareness to reading acquisition has been established, independent of the status of the opposite causal link."[36] Cited as evidence are the studies I have reviewed so far and another by Swedish psychologist Margit Torneus.

Phonological Training Does Not Translate to Reading

Torneus conducted two experiments, the first of which produced a model of the "critical importance" of phonological abilities for the development of reading and spelling, but it does not need to be discussed here because it was merely a speculative theoretical model. Although the model was a "powerful tool," the authors said, it could not prove causality "in a strict sense" regardless of what "sophisticated statistical refinements" it made. Only through "high quality" data and data analysis could conclusions about causality be drawn.[37]

This was the aim of the second experiment, in which Torneus first designed a training program to investigate the "causal relationship" between phonological ability and reading and spelling.[38] Comparing first graders who received phonological training with those who did not, the researcher found *no* statistically significant different scores between the groups in tests of phonological ability, reading, and spelling, although the experimental group did show greater improvement in phonological abilities. What the study did demonstrate is the opposite of what has been claimed: no superior reading achievement is gained from such training.

"Superior Reading Achievement"?

Also cited as evidence of the causal effects of phonemic-awareness training was research done by Swedish psychologists Ake Olofsson and Ingvar Lundberg.[39] Using Swedish kindergartners, whose usual education is made up of "a fairly low degree of structure and a pronounced emphasis on social and aesthetic development in playful settings,"[40] the researchers looked at the relationships between phonological awareness training in kindergarten and reading achievement in the first grade.

Before discussing the results, a comment about the design of this study is necessary. Because of the Swedish kindergarten curriculum, the control group—at least as described in the paper—had *no* literacy program at all. Therefore, the study provided no basis for drawing conclusions about the effectiveness of phonemic-awareness training compared with other approaches to literacy learning in kindergarten.

The first-grade follow-up found the training effect was "most salient on phonemic awareness tasks in school," but the same could not be said for silent reading, spelling, and reading nonsense and phonetically irregular words. For these, the trained and control groups had no significant test score differences at the end of first grade.[41] Furthermore, the control group children who were nonreaders in kindergarten scored significantly better on the silent reading test than did the children in the experimental groups, and the silent reading scores of the control children were in the average range of the test norms, whereas those of the experimental group children were substantially below these norms.

One can hardly say this study provides compelling evidence or indeed any kind of evidence for the claim that the training program led to "superior reading achievement."[42]

"Evidence" Versus Citations

If the premise about the causal role of phonological awareness is accepted in Stanovich's model, all else readily follows: the reader who gets off to a fast start will read more and become an even better reader; the slow starting reader will become an even worse reader; and over time, their reading achievement will continue to diverge.

The problem with this influential model is that, as we have discussed here, its critical initial premise is not substantiated, leaving the causal premises as mere speculation. A constant refrain on behalf of this explanation is science, science, science. Purportedly, it is science upon which the model and appeals for skills-based beginning reading instruction are based. By any reasonable scientific standard, however, we have a body of research from the 1980s that offers a conclusion unsupported by data, and some of the data show the opposite of what is claimed.

This literature reveals a fabrication of evidence devised in part through the *appearance* of citation strength in which quantity of studies is assumed to equal quality, multiple assertions by authorities is assumed to demonstrate strength of scientific evidence, and the repetition of citations by these authorities is assumed to equal a justified expert consensus. I am not suggesting that the fabrication is a deliberate deception. Rather, I use the term *fabrication* to mean construction and am proposing that the view of what counts as evidence has helped create a structure of ideas that serve to misrepresent the evidence. Whatever minor criticism of this research accompanies the citations is effaced by the process in which the agglomeration of a series of studies with skimpy methods and results is believed to total more than the sum of the deficient parts.

Conclusion

The research reviewed above is the background—the foundation—upon which today's research and arguments on behalf of skills-emphasis instruction rests. To repeat, I have focused on the work of Keith Stanovich because it has been the theoretical and empirical grounding of skills-emphasis research and arguments. The fundamental premise of the model Stanovich proposed in his "Matthew Effects" paper and reiterated in later papers by him and others was not, I have argued, forged in scientific evidence. It might be, of course, that later research provides the evidence previously lacking. In the chapters ahead, this possibility will be addressed.

In a later paper, Stanovich talked about believing in "letting scientific evidence answer questions" about learning to read.[43] Cited in his discussion of scientific evidence were his publications that I have discussed in this chapter.

In 1998, prominent researchers on phonemic awareness wrote, "faced with an alphabetic script, a child's level of phonemic awareness on entering school is widely held to be the strongest single determinant of the success that she or he will experience in learning to read—or conversely, the likelihood that she or he will fail."[44] Cited in support of this statement was Stanovich's "Matthew Effects" paper.

CLAIM

Difficulty understanding that words are made up of sounds and learning the "alphabetic principle" (associating sounds with alphabet letters) are the primary causes of poor reading.

WHAT THE RESEARCH ACTUALLY SHOWS

☐ Beginning reading instruction that focused on the alphabetic principle and phonics failed to produce significant benefits in word reading.

☐ Children trained in phonological awareness made significantly greater gains in phonemic awareness and nonword reading but not in sentence and paragraph comprehension or in spelling.

☐ Training in phonological awareness did not bring poor readers up to average grade-level reading.

☐ Kindergarten training in phonological awareness did not produce significantly superior reading in later grades.

☐ Skills-emphasis researchers critiquing a "meaning-based" reading program (ostensibly a whole language program) were unaware that whole language proponents had themselves, several years before the study, strongly criticized the program as the antithesis of whole language instruction that emphasizes meaning.

2

Creating "the Culprit"

Whether in formal reports by professional educators; statements by advocacy groups; testimony before federal, state, and local legislators; or the decisions of school policy makers, the basis for all current appeals for skills-emphasis teaching is a body of research funded by the NICHD, a division of the National Institutes of Health. The research is supported by the Child Development and Behavior Branch of the NICHD and is usually referred to as "the NICHD research."

The NICHD-supported reading research extends over thirty years, but the studies most frequently cited are studies conducted over the last decade. In the words of G. Reid Lyon, chief of the NICHD branch that funds the research situated in eighteen university sites across the country, and Jack Fletcher, a leading NICHD researcher, "the NICHD research supports a prominent role for explicit instruction in phonics and phonological awareness skills (i.e., alphabetic principle) for beginning reading instruction, particularly for children at risk for reading failure."[1]

Keith Stanovich may be the major theoretician of skills-first teaching, but its leading protagonist is Reid Lyon, who regularly speaks to audiences from California to Rhode Island, writes for newspapers and professional journals, testifies before federal and state legislators, appears on television and radio, and is quoted in newspaper and magazine articles. He explained to a U.S. House of Representatives committee considering an educational bill that embraces skills-first instruction:

> What our NICHD research has taught us is that in order for a beginning reader to learn how to connect or translate printed symbols (letter and letter patterns) into sound, the would-be reader must understand that our speech can be represented by printed forms (phonics). This understanding that written

spellings systematically represent the phonemes or spoken words (termed the alphabetic principle) is absolutely necessary for the development of accurate and rapid word reading skills.[2]

Although comprehension and meaning are included as necessary parts of beginning reading, the majority of Lyon's testimony—as in all his publications and presentations—is on phonemic awareness, phonics, decoding, the alphabetic principle, and phonemes. Moreover, when comprehension is mentioned, the emphasis remains on the mastery of skills that he contends beget it:

> Our research continues to converge on the following findings. Good readers are phonemically aware, understand the alphabetic principle, can apply these skills to the development and application of phonics skills when reading and spelling words, and can accomplish these applications in a fluent and accurate manner. Given the ability to rapidly and automatically decode and recognize words, good readers bring strong vocabularies and good syntactic and grammatical skills to the reading comprehension process.[3]

What, in Lyon's view, is the element separating good and poor readers?

> In contrast to good readers who understand that segmented units of speech can be linked to letters and letter patterns, poor readers have substantial difficulty in developing this "alphabetic principle." The culprit appears to be a deficit in phonemic awareness—the understanding that words are made up of sound segments called phonemes.[4]

Lyon's own writing and much of the NICHD research do not merely investigate phonemic awareness and related skills; their goal has also been the repudiation of whole language. For example, Lyon criticizes prominent whole language educators for allegedly rejecting "explicit instruction" and for maintaining that meaning-emphasis teaching is sufficient for ensuring that children learn to decode and recognize unfamiliar words. He goes on to assert that "scientific research, however, simply does not support the claim that context and authentic text are a proxy for decoding skills."[5] Commenting on a quote from Kenneth Goodman, a major whole language scholar, Lyon writes, "some advocates of whole language practices who are opposed to putting an emphasis on phonological awareness skills, phonics skills, and word-recognition processes have done many students a disservice."[6]

Whether the NICHD and related research on beginning reading actually supports current arguments made on behalf of skills-first teaching is the subject of this and the chapters that follow. As in the previous chapter, the research I have chosen to examine here is the very research cited most often by those who argue for direct, explicit instruction that emphasizes skills in beginning reading.

A "Remedial Intervention Protocol"

Reid Lyon and NICHD-supported researcher Louisa Moats explain that intervention studies have been a significant part of the NICHD research because they help document the causal role of phonemic awareness and related skills, demonstrate how training in these skills facilitates learning to read, and contribute to the creation of effective "intervention protocols."[7] One important intervention study they cite for these claims was led by prominent NICHD-supported researcher Barbara Foorman.[8]

The study used second- and third-grade students who were "reading disabled" and compared a "sight-word," or "whole-word," training program with two kinds of phonics programs. The sight-word program taught students 150 individual words plus endings. One of the phonics groups used a "systematic, step-by-step" synthetic phonics approach in which the children first learned to connect letter names and sounds and then learned to blend phonemes into words.[9] The second phonics group was taught analytic phonics in which words were learned through "onset" (first letter) and "rime" (rhyme ending) patterns (/b/ig, /p/ig, /d/ig) rather than phonics rules. Each group did a variety of writing, reading, and spelling activities to reinforce the respective teaching. The training took place each day for an hour.

At the end of the year, the synthetic phonics group exceeded the analytic phonics group and the sight-word group on tests of phonological analysis, but because the groups were not matched in verbal IQ, ethnicity, and social class, the respective scores could not readily be attributed to differences in the training programs. The researchers observed that one reason for the synthetic phonics group's superior scores could have been that half of these children attended a school "in a more affluent neighborhood." Given these and other differences—the synthetic phonics group had higher IQ test scores, for example—the researchers themselves acknowledged that "it seems plausible that uncontrolled demographic and other participant characteristics may mediate treatment effects on phonological and orthographic processing."[10]

Perhaps more critical is the reported fact that regardless of the differences in phonological abilities, the lack of significant group differences on the word-reading test showed that these abilities did not "transfer to gains in word reading."[11] The researchers did not explain why they did not use the paragraph comprehension portion of the test (the Woodcock-Johnson Psychoeducational Battery—Revised), a test that would have provided another—and more independent—measure of reading progress among the three groups for whom comprehension was not a direct part of the training program.

Why the researchers used sight-word teaching as a foil for phonics-training programs is not clear because there appears to be unanimity among both skills-first and whole language educators that the approach does not work well. Regardless, given the lack of significant differences in word-reading gains among the groups and the personal and demographic characteristics that restricted interpreting the results, it is not clear how the study contributes to Lyon and Moats' formulation of "remedial intervention protocols."[12]

From Skills to Word Reading?

Other "preventive and remedial intervention protocols" cited by Lyon and Moats[13] were devised by NICHD-supported psychologists Joseph Torgesen and Richard Wagner. Kindergartners who had low scores on tests of letter-name knowledge and phonological awareness were divided into four instructional groups. One received phonological awareness training and synthetic phonics instruction (PASP). That is, in addition to teaching sounds in words, their instruction provided "explicit instruction in letter/sound correspondences" and in applying this knowledge to decoding words. A second group, called Embedded Phonics (EP), received phonological awareness and phonics instruction as required within reading and spelling activities. The instruction was direct but was employed only as the need for it arose in the context of literacy work. A third group was in a "regular classroom" and received individual tutorial instruction to support the regular classroom reading program (RCS). And the fourth group was a "no-treatment control" group of children who received no extra tutorial support.[14] Supposedly, classroom teaching was guided by a whole language philosophy.

Follow-up tests after two and a half years, when the students were in second grade, found that on a measure of "word attack" (phonics) skills, the PASP group had scores significantly higher than those of the two other tutored groups and higher yet than the group that received no tutoring. However, on a test of word identification, "the substantially superior alphabetic reading skills of children in the PASP group did not produce a corresponding advantage in real word reading."[15] The researchers themselves observed that this pattern had been found in other studies. Summarizing these results, and apparently undeterred by the findings and statements of the researchers, Fletcher and Lyon stated that the PASP group "had much stronger reading skills than the children in all the other groups."[16]

It is not clear what the study was trying to examine or demonstrate. Presumably, it was primarily concerned with the question of whether extra tutoring in phonological awareness and phonics of one form or another makes a difference. The fundamental question in which the study remains mired, however, is "Difference in what?" The "what" is classroom teaching, which is only superficially described. The researchers asked the teachers to "place their instructional approach on a 5-point continuum from 1 (phonics oriented) to 5 (whole language), and the majority in each of the four groups responded either with 3 or 4."[17]

The authors note that the self-ratings were consistent with their "observations that regular classroom reading instruction was primarily literature based and guided by a whole language philosophy, with phonics being taught on an as-needed basis rather than systematically," but beyond this they offer nothing more about classroom teaching.[18]

Group differences were also found in grade retention. During the course of the study, about 26 percent of the children were retained in either kindergarten or first grade. The respective rates of retention were: PASP group, 9 percent; EP, 25 percent; RCS, 30 percent; and the no-treatment group (no tutoring of any kind) had a retention rate of 41 percent. It is not clear why any of the children were retained at all, since at the end of kindergarten and first grade there were no significant differences in "real-word reading ability," as measured by the "word identification" test. It appears that children might have been retained because of their lower word-attack scores, even though no statistically significant association was found at the end of second grade between these scores and reading comprehension or word identification. Indeed, since the lower retention rate of the PASP group seems to have less to do with their reading development, it could be concluded that the retention was motivated by the school's *belief* that phonetic ability is a predictor of future reading achievement.

Torgesen, Wagner, and their colleagues have cautioned that they have not "really verified" that their intervention programs "will make a permanent and significant difference in long-term reading outcomes."[19] They also point out that theirs is not the only research that has failed to obtain a training benefit. Another study, by Canadian psychologist Maureen Lovett and her colleagues, for example, found that a group trained in phonological skills made better gains in measures of phonological awareness, but these gains did not transfer to word identification, passage comprehension, or spelling—indeed, on measures of these abilities, the groups performed about the same.[20] Torgesen and his colleagues note that although training programs might "eventually produce complete remediation of the phonetic reading-skill deficit, in the absence of direct evidence we simply do not know if this assumption is correct."[21]

"The Primary Phenotypic Manifestation"

Lyon and Moats extend their explanation of reading by asserting that the chief sign of a reading disability is an inability to read single words out of context, such as in a list of words, especially when they are novel (such as phonetically irregular words like *come* and *sure*) or pseudowords (*gop, teg*). As they put it, "It is generally accepted among reading scientists that the primary phenotypic manifestation of developmental reading disability (RD) is inaccurate and dysfluent decoding of single words out of context." A main reason for these problems, they explain, is that "children with reading problems cannot rapidly and accurately link sounds to symbols in an alphabetic orthography."[22]

This statement has the trappings of an erudite, scientifically based conclusion but is no more than what anyone who has observed someone with reading trouble knows: a person who does not know basic words has an especially hard time identifying words that do not conform to regular phonetic patterns and mastering sound-symbol correspondences to identify words that conform to phonetically regular patterns. It is a considerable leap, however, to conclude that these are the causes of the reading problems. The fact is, behavioral symptoms do not explain the causes of that behavior.

As evidence of their interpretation, Lyon and Moats cite the work of Richard Olson and his colleagues that looked at word-recognition ability. Their training study differed from most others in its use of a talking computer system that provided speech support for children's decoding difficulties. Two groups of poor readers in second through fifth grade read stories on a computer and received help with word pronunciation and decoding when they encountered difficult words. While one group received explicit training in phonological awareness (PA group), the other group read stories and practiced "comprehension strategies of prediction, question generation, clarification and summarization" (CS group). The CS group had twice as much print exposure as the PA group. The difference between the two groups, therefore, was in a training emphasis on phonemic analysis for one and on comprehension for the other.[23]

At the end of the training period, although the phonological awareness group had made significantly greater gains in phonemic awareness and nonword reading, there were *no* statistically significant differences between the groups in sentence and paragraph comprehension or in spelling. Moreover, although the groups did not differ on an untimed test of word recognition, the comprehension strategies group had significantly better scores on a timed test of word recognition, a test in which the phonological awareness children "sometimes sounded out difficult words too slowly to figure them out within 2 seconds."[24]

One year after the training period ended, the phonological awareness group did better on tests of phonemic awareness and phonics (nonword reading), but the group's "superiority in these skills again *did not* result in more rapid gains in word recognition tests." For example, on a timed test of word recognition, there was "virtually no group difference in follow-up gains."[25]

This lack of significant group differences in tests of word recognition and reading achievement remained at the two-year follow-up. Here too the researchers observed, "the more explicit phonologically based programs produced better phonological decoding, but not significantly better word recognition in most measures at the end of training." Furthermore, neither training condition was sufficient for bringing the children up to average grade-level reading: both remained "well below the national norms [for their grades] at the end of training and at follow-up."[26]

Alternative Explanations of Data

Lyon and Moats cite another study that, ironically, could be used to draw opposite conclusions—as could some of the studies we have already reviewed—about the relationship between decoding and reading disability. Australian psychologists Anne Castles and Max Coltheart gave poor readers and normal readers between eight and fourteen years of age three lists to read: one of phonetically regular words (*take, free*), another of irregular words (*blood, shoe*), and a third of phonetically regular nonsense words (*sut, lif*).[27]

On the whole, the poor readers did much better identifying the phonetically regular than the irregular and nonsense words. Out of 30 words for each category, their average identification scores were: 20.4 regular words, 11.3 irregular words, and 12.9 nonsense words. From children's different test scores, Castles and Coltheart identified two types of problems: a word identification/memory problem evident in children who had more problems naming irregular than regular words and a phonological processing problem apparent in children who had more problems naming nonsense words than irregular ones.

Missing here is a third interpretation: poor readers did better identifying the regular words because these words provided *both* meaning and sound-symbol relationships to draw upon. Thus, the data suggest that when poor readers have both meaning and sound-symbol information, they do much better than when they are able to apply only their ability with sound-symbol relationships. Similarly, the data suggest that the more meaning is brought to a word-identification task, the more likely a poor reader will identify the word. It could further be concluded, of course, that the lack of full written language contexts for the words prevented the poor readers from testing their sound-symbol "guesstimates."

Reaching the "Average Range" in Reading Norms

A study by NICHD-supported psychologist Frank Vellutino and his colleagues provided tutoring for poor readers in the first grade for thirty minutes a day. Half the session was devoted to reading books "for meaning and fun," during which comprehension, decoding, word identification, and other reading skills were taught. In other words, various skills were taught in context. The remaining time was devoted to sight vocabulary, phoneme awareness, phonetic decoding, and writing, as "determined by the child's individual needs."[28] In a discussion of this study in their review of NICHD-reading research, Reid Lyon and Jack Fletcher describe the reading-for-meaning-and-fun portion of the tutoring as time "devoted to activities involving decoding and other strategies for word recognition," thereby making the half of the training session that resembled a whole language approach seem more like direct instruction.[29]

Lyon and Fletcher go on to report the results, saying that "at the end of only one semester, approximately 70 percent of the children were reading within or above the average range based on national norms."[30] This description, too, is a misrepresentation. In addition to the tutored group just described, other children received tutoring through their school that was not directed by the researchers. This tutoring "varied markedly from school to school and included everything from individually tailored one-to-one remediation (that was quite similar to the remediation provided by research staff) to 'small' group instruction (sometimes 9 or 10 children in a group) using a highly structured basal approach." The children received this school-based tutoring "typically 3 days a week," not daily like the research-tutored group.[31]

Essentially, the two individually tutored groups had similar achievement: 44.7 percent of the research-tutored children were in the 45th percentile-or-above range in reading achievement at the end of first grade, compared with approximately 43.8 percent of children who received school-based tutoring. Dramatically lower was the 19.2 percent of those in small-group instruction who were at this percentile range.

Complicating an interpretation of the results are the differences in the number of days of tutoring each of the two groups received—every day for one, approximately three days for the other—and in the range of sizes of the groups—from one to nine or ten. Here, even the questionably superior achievement of both individually tutored groups over that of the small groups suggests more about the influence of individual instruction than about particular aspects of instruction. One interpretation that did seem clear was the lack of straight correlations between phonological awareness and reading achievement: students with low reading achievement "performed as well as or better" on phoneme segmentation tests as did good or very good readers.[32]

"Improved Reading Abilities"

An NICHD study with inner-city kindergartners that has been described by other NICHD-supported researchers as showing that "children who receive training in phoneme awareness demonstrate improved reading abilities in first grade and beyond"[33] was headed by reading researcher Susan Brady. These children were compared with other kindergartners in classes that "followed the usual curriculum which adopted a 'whole language' approach designed to foster interest in literacy."[34]

At the end of kindergarten, "no significant differences were found in any of the posttest achievement measures," that is, "comparable gains were made by the trained and control groups in letter knowledge, reading and spelling."[35] The one difference was on two phonological measures in which the training group did perform significantly better than the control group.

Despite this similarity, an inexplicable school decision was made. Although the groups "had been comparable" at the end of kindergarten "on both achievement (letter knowledge, reading, spelling, math) and general aptitude measures, not all of the children had been promoted to first grade." Three of the twenty-one children from the phoneme-training group "were put in pre-one classes, rather than in first grade, while ten of the twenty-one children from the control classes were placed in pre-one classes." In a footnote, the researchers stated that "because of the confidentiality of teacher records," they could not determine if the promotion pattern reflected "teacher difference in inclination to retain/promote or a distinct pattern for this particular year." The researchers could have made their own judgments, based on their extensive test results, about whether the children should have been promoted, but they did not. How much promotion was based on the beliefs of teachers—who themselves had provided the training program—that the trained children had a satisfactory foundation for advancing to first grade regardless of the test results is not known.[36]

For the students retained in pre-one classes, as the researchers themselves observed, "the extent of reading instruction and writing activities" was "likely to be less than in first grade." Consequently, although at the end of first grade the children who had been in the phoneme-training program "performed significantly better" on the word-identification and word-attack tests, the curriculum differences impaired any interpretation of these results. Recognizing this, the researchers compared the scores of only those children who had been promoted to first grade—eighteen from the phoneme-training group and eleven from the control group—and found that neither group of test scores "reached [statistical] significance."[37]

In short, neither at the end of kindergarten nor first grade were there statistically significant differences in reading measures favoring the children who had been in the phonological awareness–training program.

The Failure of "Meaning-Based" Teaching

Discussing the advantage of "code-based" instruction over "meaning based" instruction (a coded term the skills-emphasis literature often uses for whole language instruction), Lyon and Fletcher[38] cite research by psychologists Rebecca Brown and Rebecca Felton that describes code-emphasis instruction as teaching relationships between letters and sounds and stressing "the use of word-specific information (i.e., sound-symbol relationship) for word identification." Meaning-emphasis instruction, in contrast, according to them, "focuses on teaching the child to process text for meaning" and stresses "context and picture cues."[39] Using these "guidelines," the researchers selected the Houghton Mifflin reading program[40] as their "meaning emphasis, or Context, approach and the Lippincott Basic Reading program[41] as the Code approach."[42]

At the end of both first and second grades, the children in the code group had higher achievement scores in word attack, word identification, passage comprehension, and spelling, leading the researchers to conclude that code instruction was more beneficial than meaning-emphasis instruction and that children should receive intensive, direct instruction in "language analysis" and the "alphabetic code."[43] In their summary of the research, Fletcher and Lyon repeat this conclusion about the "significantly higher mean scores" of children taught with code-based instruction than those of children taught with meaning-based instruction.[44]

Omitted from these conclusions is the critique of both the meaning-based program (the Houghton Mifflin reading program) and code program (Lippincott) by whole language supporters Kenneth Goodman, Patrick Shannon, Yvonne Freeman, and Sharon Murphy in their 1988 book *Report Card on Basal Readers*. Brown, Felton, Lyon, and Fletcher might regard the Houghton Mifflin program as meaning-based, but for Goodman and his coauthors, it is not. They criticize Houghton Mifflin and similar programs for having "more concern with controlling the sequence of sounds, words, and skills than in providing authentic language in texts." Rather than being meaning-based, Goodman and his colleagues contended, the lessons are "keyed to practicing skills. The story is a means of focusing on and practicing the skills and learning the words, which are the real object of instruction." Goodman and his coauthors also single out the Houghton Mifflin program for claiming to teach children how to think about the strategies needed to do a task (metacognition) but actually doing no more than controlling their thinking so that they will arrive at the "right" answer. "The view that learning must be controlled" turns "metacognition, a property of the learner" into "a property of the program."[45] Fletcher and Lyon, rendering *meaning-based* as a stand-in for *whole language,* apparently were unaware that the program—which through the research findings presumably damned whole language—had itself been criticized by whole language supporters as "un-whole language" five years before the Felton and Brown research was published and a decade before Fletcher and Lyon wrote their essay.

Conclusion

The studies I have reviewed here are among the prominent studies in the NICHD reading research. They are among the evidential citations of the chief of the NICHD funding division, who refers to them in his publications and in speeches on the contributions from researchers supported by his division. Lyon has referred to them in his testimony on federal and state literacy legislation and policy and has discussed them in special issues of journals devoted to skills-emphasis teaching. They have also been repeatedly cited by others writing in support of skills-emphasis teaching. Astonishingly, despite the failure of this work to demonstrate the purported causal effect of phonemic-awareness skills, this line of research continues both to be cited as evidence of this causal explanation and to be used to overturn promising and effective reform in the name of scientifically verifiable practices.

If one looks closely enough at portrayals of the NICHD research, some self-criticism can be found. For instance, Lyon and Moats acknowledge that "It is also critical to recognize that in all of the NICHD intervention studies to date, improvements in decoding and word reading accuracy have been far easier to obtain than improvements in reading fluency and automaticity."[46] Such admissions, however, are brief and rare and are quickly followed by hypotheses of why a transfer did not occur.

Similarly, although discussions of the NICHD research always state that the "intervention research" involves both "explicit teaching of phonics" and a "balanced approach" that includes "good literature" and "reading for enjoyment," a review of this research reveals that these latter facets of literacy learning and anything resembling "balance" have been given more lip service than actual experimental attention.[47] Expressions of concern for balance are never more than tangential to the studies and summary essays on the studies.

The relentless claim is about what "our NICHD studies have taught us"[48] about the causal effects of phonological awareness on reading, and statements such as the following are near-ceaseless: "From an empirical standpoint, there is a wealth of evidence that deficits in phonological awareness not only co-occur with deficits in basic reading skills but that the relationship is, in fact, a causal one, with deficits in phonological awareness impeding the acquisition of reading skills."[49] In the chapters ahead, we will review additional NICHD research cited in support of this claim.

CLAIM

Children taught with the Open Court beginning reading program, which emphasizes the direct, systematic instruction of phonemic awareness and phonics skills, had test scores on word skills, word identification, and reading comprehension that were superior to those of children taught with a whole language approach.

WHAT THE RESEARCH ACTUALLY SHOWS

☐ When the comprehension and word skills (word identification, decoding) scores are analyzed by the classrooms and schools in which the groups were instructed, with the exception of one Open Court school and one whole language school, the scores of the two groups among the schools were comparable.

☐ The extreme, atypical scores—very high in a single school using Open Court and very low in a single school using whole language—produced the differences in overall group mean scores and thereby masked the otherwise similar achievement outcomes when examined by school-based results.

☐ Although the research claims to have used whole language instruction for a comparison group, the published research paper offers insufficient information to determine if this was so.

☐ The extraordinary publicity given this study for more than a year prior to its publication was not justified by the actual research results.

3

The Foorman Study

"M—M—M—M." "Ma—Ma—Ma—Ma." "Mad—Mad—Mad—Mad." Chanted in unison, these exercises were part of the reading lessons in classroom after classroom in an elementary school in Sacramento City, California. Additional chants responded to teacher questions about what letters were needed to change *mad* into *made, made* to *make,* and *make* to *Mike.* The lessons were part of a new reading program called Open Court, the hope of many educators and parents in the Sacramento City school district who wanted to reverse "years of substandard achievement" caused primarily, they believed, by whole language teaching. In contrast, Open Court was described as "a systematic, phonics-based language arts program" that used heavily scripted instructional guides complete with daily lesson plans. In the words of one teacher, the teachers manual "is so specific, you really can't miss it." The program was especially good for new teachers, said one principal, because "they need much more scripting" than had been provided by previous programs. For principals, the program made supervision easier because instruction was uniform.[1]

Beyond these professional appraisals, the district had chosen the program—as had numerous districts across the nation—based on research purportedly demonstrating its success "with poor, urban student populations." NICHD-supported research done in the Houston, Texas, schools had "pitted Open Court against two other programs, one of which used a whole language approach and the other a less explicit phonics approach," that is, phonics was learned through reading materials with phonetically consistent words, but the phonics elements were not taught as separate lessons. After a year, the study reported, the children using Open Court had superior scores on reading tests.[2]

The study has received extensive publicity and has been acclaimed by partisans of skill-emphasis instruction as the premier research to date supporting their principles. Reported in the media throughout North America and spotlighted in a national report on reading, the study has been used to justify local and state educational policy and state and federal legislation mandating the direct instruction of skills in beginning reading education.

"Direct Code" Versus "Implicit Code"

Headed by psychologist Barbara Foorman, the study, commonly called "the Foorman study," compared three different beginning reading teaching approaches to see which was most effective in advancing the reading achievement of Title 1 students who were poor readers (Title 1 refers to federal funding provided for poor children with low academic achievement).[3] Although three different approaches were compared, the comparison between Open Court and whole language was central in the researchers' interpretation and in subsequent school policy discussions and decisions. All teachers received both preservice training the summer prior to the research year and supervision during the year. As an adjunct to classroom instruction, children were tutored for thirty minutes each day, either one to one or in small groups of three to five students.

The specifics are these: Open Court emphasized training in phonemic awareness and phonics and used "decodable texts"—books composed of words that are phonetically regular and constructed from phonics elements children have previously learned—to reinforce these skills. Storybooks were used to develop "skills in oral language comprehension and love of story." Spelling dictation exercises moved students "from phonetic spellings toward conventional spelling based on phonics knowledge and spelling conventions. Writing workshop activities and anthologies of fiction, nonfiction, and poetry are introduced by mid-Grade 1." This description might suggest a program with a variety of literacy activities, but for the researchers the constituent key in early reading development was and is the explicit, *direct* teaching of the alphabetic code. Hence, the Open Court instruction was called "direct code."[4]

"Embedded code" classrooms also taught phonemic awareness and phonics, but these skills were "embedded" in (part of) the reading and writing materials and activities, such as books that use repeated instances of phonics and spelling patterns ("predictable books"). Other spelling activities served to reinforce and extend the phonics patterns. For example, *-at, -on,* and *-ing* served as basic patterns from which words could be extended or substituted: *bat, cat, mat; ring, sing, wing.*

Whole language was the term used to describe the third group and the control group. It was labeled "implicit code" teaching because phonological awareness, phonics, and other word skills were taught as part of reading activities that emphasized meaning and a "print-rich environment" in which teachers served as facilitators rather than as directors of learning. During reading, the instructor taught specific skills that were part of (implicit in) the reading materials, but the instruction was "incidental to the act of making meaning from print." The skills were not taught separately and directly. The term *implicit code* represented the researchers' hypothesis about the chief causal influence in learning to read—that is, the alphabet code had to be taught directly, not implicitly.[5]

The differences between the whole language groups were first, that research teachers were trained by the research staff, while the control group teachers "were trained and supervised by district personnel"; and, second, only the research students were tutored. The researchers had intended to use the control group to determine if tutoring made a difference but because most of these children were in a school that had the highest percentage of poor children—71 percent of the children were eligible for the federal lunch program—and that school was regarded as a "tough" one, the researchers did not use the group as a comparison in its final published report.[6]

At the end of the year, Foorman and her colleagues reported, the direct code students did statistically better than students in the other instructional groups in a measure of decoding using tests of letter-word identification and word-attack skills. These students also did better in tests of phonological processing and word reading.

Presumably, these differences should have been accompanied by similar test scores on spelling and reading comprehension; however, like research outcomes discussed in the previous chapter, this did not happen: no statistically significant group differences were found on the spelling subtest of the Kaufman Test of Educational Achievement[7] or on two comprehension tests. On the Passage Comprehension subtest of the Woodcock-Johnson—Revised,[8] the direct code group had a standard score of 96.7, compared with the 92.0 of the whole language group, a difference that the researchers said was "not significant."

In a fine example of scientific rigor, this conclusion was qualified by the observation that the lack of significance was due to a conservative statistical method meant to minimize the possibility of concluding that results are significant when they are not ("Type 1" errors). When a less-stringent standard was used, the researchers pointed out, the "mean differences" on this test "were large," favoring the direct code group, of course.[9]

Woodcock-Johnson (R) Passage Comprehension Test

One can argue against this recasting of the findings by asking why stringent statistical standards were used in the first place and then dismissed when the results did not accord with the researchers' expectations. In a similar vein, we may wonder just how large the magnitude of difference was in the recalculation.

If we go beyond the group scores—something the researchers did not do in their published report—we have another potential method of examining the scores and the effectiveness of the respective teaching approaches. Thanks to the researchers, I was able to obtain the original data, which enabled me to examine the achievement scores in each of the schools in the study. In this way I was able to make a more detailed comparison of reading achievement.

The teaching approaches were divided among several schools, with some having only one approach and others having two or three. In each grade in each school, one or more classes was used for each approach. For purposes of concentrating on the central comparison of Open Court versus whole language, I have omitted the embedded phonics approach in this analysis, but have added the nontutored whole language class in one school that had both tutored Open Court and tutored whole language classes. This allows comparison of alternative whole language teaching in a school not designated as "tough."

The following chart compares Passage Comprehension scores by teaching approach, school, and grade:

Whole Language (tutored)	Open Court	Whole Language (nontutored)
	First Grade	
92.1 (school 2)	92.0 (school 7)	
93.6 (school 6)	92.5 (school 4)	
95.5 (school 8)	100.4 (school 6)	
	112.2 (school 5)	
	Second Grade	
95.8 (school 6)	93.3 (school 6)	95.9 (school 6)
83.1 (school 2)	89.0 (school 7)	
96.2 (school 8)		

The chart shows:

- Most of the schools' standard scores for all three teaching approaches were in the 90s. Six of the seven whole language grades (combining three tutored first grades, three tutored second grades, and one nontutored second grade) have scores similar to those of five of the six Open Court grades (four first grade, two second grade). Overall, this school comparison provides little striking evidence of the superiority of the Open Court instruction. Although there were two "extreme" scores—112.2 for Open Court in first grade (school 5) and 83.1 for whole language in second grade (school 2)—the majority of scores does not show any substantial differences among teaching approaches when examined by grade-score outcomes. The first-grade scores (93.6 and 92.1) for whole language in two schools were essentially the same as those for Open Court in two schools (92.5 and 92.0). The 95.5 average whole language first-grade score was slightly better than two Open Court first-grade score outcomes and not very distant from the Open Court score of 100.4 in school 6.

- Only the first-grade Open Court score of 112.2 in school 5 was significantly beyond the average range of both whole language and Open Court scores in both grades in all schools. This higher score came from two classrooms in the school in which the scores of the students were uncharacteristically uniform, unlike the considerably varied student scores in all other classrooms and schools. It is *the scores from the two classes in this single school* that elevated the overall average of the Open Court passage comprehension scores reported in the published paper. The "direction" and "magnitude" of the differences that the researchers maintained were reflected in the overall achievement scores are not found in comparisons across grades in the schools. The difference between overall scores and particular grade scores is especially striking for the second grade in which two of the three tutored whole language scores were *higher* (95.8 and 96.2) than the Open Court scores (93.3 and 89.0).

- Moreover, the 95.9 score of the second-grade whole language students in school 6, who did not receive tutoring, was *higher* than both Open Court second-grade scores.

- The extremely low score of 83.1 in the whole language second grade in school 2 had the converse effect of the extremely high Open Court score: it lowered the overall whole language comprehension score reported in the published paper.

- The high Open Court first-grade score of 112.2 and the very low whole language second-grade score of 83.1 suggest that this divergence might have been influenced by something other than the teaching approach—possibly by tracking or teaching differences between or within the schools. Since the published research report fails to note this divergence, it obviously did not provide information to explain it.

- Overall, *neither* teaching approach had a satisfactory impact on comprehension for most of the students. No explanation can be deduced from the published report on how this happened because the article provides little information about the teaching and learning that occurred in classrooms or the effect that influences inside or outside the school might have had on teaching and learning.

"Basic Reading Cluster" Test

We will now turn to the results of another measure, the Woodcock-Johnson (R) Basic Reading Cluster, composed of letter-identification, word-identification, and word-attack (pronouncing pseudowords such as *dif, giz, dop,* and *blif*) subtests. As we have seen in other studies, skills-emphasis proponents use these kinds of skills often as the "gold standard" gauges to justify skills-emphasis instruction. As Foorman and her colleagues say, the Reading Cluster "represents a measure of decoding."

The investigators concluded that the Reading Cluster results showed "significant instructional group effects" favoring the direct code group over the implicit code (whole language) group (the respective average scores were 96.1 and 89.6).[10] As we did with the previous section, we will again look beyond these overall group averages and examine the grade scores, which can be seen in the following chart.

Whole Language (tutored)	Open Court	Whole Language (nontutored)
	First Grade	
90.0 (school 2)	93.6 (school 7)	
90.4 (school 6)	91.4 (school 4)	
100.2 (school 8)	100.0 (school 6)	
	112.6 (school 5)	
	Second Grade	
93.0 (school 6)	91.3 (school 6)	
79.6 (school 2)	85.8 (school 7)	88.0 (school 6)
91.1 (school 8)		

- Like the pattern of the comprehension test results, the two first-grade direct code (Open Court) classes in school 5 was considerably higher and that provided researchers with an elevated overall direct code average group score. Conversely, for implicit code (whole language), the exceptionally low scores of the second graders in school 2 reduced the overall implicit code average group score.
- If we were to set aside the two extreme scores, we would see that at first grade, the results were comparable for both kinds of instruction, and at second grade, two whole language scores were actually better than one of the direct code scores and similar to the other.
- The implicit code students who had no tutoring did better than the second-grade Open Court students in school 7.

Like the comprehension test results, except for the two extreme scores, school performances on these measures of decoding are comparable. This raises the questions: Why did Foorman and her colleagues not publish a by-grade and school analysis? Why did they not explain how two classes of exceptionally able students in one school both ended up in the implicit code group?

On a word-reading test at the end of the school year, 38 percent of the implicit code students could read 2.5 words or fewer out of 50. In contrast, only 17 percent of the direct code students read 2.5 words or fewer. Similar results were obtained for phonological processing. As we have already seen in other studies, superior skills in word identification and phonemic awareness did not in this study have a parallel connection with reading comprehension and spelling.

"Formal Reading Inventory" Test

The scores on the Formal Reading Inventory test (FRI)[11] were alike, with standard score averages of 81.8 for Open Court and 83.1 for whole language. Using dubious logic, the researchers attributed these very similar results to the test's "floor effect," whereby a student must reach a certain level of comprehension ability before he or she can answer a sufficient number of questions on the test and thereby obtain a score that can be differentiated from other students' scores.[12] Because most children failed to reach this floor, the tests did not discriminate among their scores, according to the researchers. The researchers also explained that the scores were "relatively low across groups because text comprehension presupposes an adequate decoding ability," which few of the students had.[13]

Regardless of the researchers' explanation, the FRI *is* normed for first and second graders, and relative to these norms the children in this study did not score well. As the test manual states, "The FRI is appropriate for students ages 6 [years]–6 [months] through 17 years who understand the directions of the test and are able to silently and orally read paragraphs."[14] The researchers' floor-effect explanation misses the point that the first and second graders used in norming the test exceeded the floor that many students in the Foorman study could not. This explanation is also puzzling, considering that when the researchers chose the FRI, they must have considered it an adequate measure of reading for their study, and they made no mention of concerns about floor effect at that time.

The Omitted Assessment

In my considerable experience in testing poor readers, I have never seen the FRI used as it was used in the Foorman study. In fact, the study must be appraised also by the portion of the FRI the researchers did *not* use to assess reading. More than a comprehension test, the FRI provides a means for analyzing a reader's errors or "miscues" that can cause comprehension problems, which is similar to the analysis of reading recommended by whole language advocates. The FRI test manual describes the instrument as an "assessment of oral reading miscues [that] provides examiners with a qualitative analysis of the students' reading performance." For example, the examiner can determine if a reader has problems with "meaning similarity" (such as *into the city* for *downtown*), "functional similarity" (*saw* for *looked*), "phonemic similarity" (*bats* for *hats*), self-corrections, omissions, additions, poor phrasing, lack of expression, nervousness, or poor attitude that could affect comprehension.[15]

This miscue portion of the FRI would have allowed the Foorman study researchers to go beyond the floor-effect explanation to gain more understanding of the processes that contributed to the comprehension test results. Their failure to do so raises the question: Did they not use it because it has a conception different from their model of what factors contribute to learning to read, a conception that includes but extends beyond phonemic awareness and decoding? Using this portion of the test could have provided them with an array of useful information but information that had the potential to nullify the reigning explanation guiding their investigation.

Meaning of *Whole Language* in the Foorman Study

In appraising the Foorman study I have so far accepted the assumption that the teaching described as whole language (implicit code) was, in fact, just that. There are reasons to question this claim, however, because the information the study provides about actual classroom practice is sparse and the researchers' essays and investigations have consistently rejected whole language theory and practice. In an Internet discussion sponsored by the National Reading Conference, Jack Fletcher, one of the Foorman study researchers, stated that "data on teacher effect" and "program specific evaluations" appeared in the Foorman study article published in the *Journal of Educational Psychology*.[16] The Foorman report, however, does not go beyond "effect" and final "evaluations," and it provides meager information at best. The primary ingredients of whole language are outlined in the published paper, but no information is provided about their implementation.

A suggestion of the extent to which whole language instruction was actually implemented can be gleaned from their description of teacher supervision:

> During the school year, the research staff visited each teacher's classroom every other week or more frequently, if necessary, to monitor implementation of instruction and to provide feedback on the quality of implementation. Instructional supervisors from the district were available at each school to help teachers with basic issues of classroom management, a resource that was called on frequently. Research staff members met with the teachers of a particular grade level at each school during their planning time to discuss instructional issues. Finally, to share instructional strategies across sites, teachers implementing a common program in different schools came together after school three times during the school year.[17]

Given this apparently high level of supervision, one wonders what the research staff made of the following: In the word-reading test, according to the researchers, the whole language first graders could read an average of less than one word in October and still less than one word in December. By February they were reading an average of slightly more than one word (2.30) compared to an average of more than 6 words for the Open Court group. What, if anything, did the researchers do in response to these deficiencies? Because the published report offers no information about what whole language meant in practice, we do not know what the supervisory response was. Nor do we know anything about the teachers' responses to the children's lack of progress. Is the conclusion to be drawn that nothing could have been done to remedy the problem because whole language teaching was steadfast and irremediable?

If we accept the description of supervision at face value, we must assume that one or more of the following occurred: (a) the children in whole language classes were relentlessly sliding into Neverland month after month, but none of the supervisors recognized this growing failure, and therefore, they offered no supervision or advice for turning things around and promoting success; (b) the supervisors recognized the growing failure but did nothing because they did not want to "interfere" with the instruction and thereby "contaminate" it—and if so, the supervision was again worthless, as in (a); or (c) the supervisors *did* attempt to intervene and improve whole language instruction, but their efforts failed because the instruction was incapable of teaching children words and word skills as well as Open Court could.

Situation (c), of course, is the scenario that the study's researchers want one to conclude. However, a true validation of interpretation (c) requires evidence that everything reasonably possible was done to ensure that whole language teachers and students obtained everything needed for the literacy goals. The evidence of this is not in the published paper.

Conclusion

In March 1998, the National Academy of Science published *Preventing Reading Difficulties in Young Children*, a report reviewing reading research and offering instructional strategies meant to accomplish the goal expressed in the title of the report.[18] Two members of the committee were Barbara Foorman and Marilyn Jager Adams, a coauthor of Open Court.

In the chapter titled "Instructional Strategies," eight pages of its twelve-page section on "First Grade: Fostering Reading in the First-Grade Classroom" is devoted to the Foorman study. After describing the "three approaches to first grade instruction"—that is, whole language, direct code (Open Court), and embedded phonics—the report concludes that the results of the Foorman study indicate

> that not all interventions are equal. The amount of improvement in word reading skill appears to be associated with the degree of explicitness in the instructional method. Furthermore, children

with higher phonological processing scores at the beginning of the year demonstrated greater improvement in word reading skills in all instructional groups. Explicit instruction in the alphabetic principle was more effective with children who began the year doing poorly in phonological processing.[19]

This paragraph concludes the twelve-page subsection. These conclusions became part of this widely publicized and discussed national report before the Foorman study was actually published. It marks an extraordinarily influential point on an unbroken trail of secondary reports that began in February 1997—more than a year before the study appeared in a professional journal—acclaiming the triumph of skills-emphasis teaching. At the start, based on Foorman's presentation of the study at the American Association for the Advancement of Science national convention, the *Toronto Globe and Mail* announced, "In what is billed as the first hard scientific comparison of whole language versus the phonics method of learning to read, a U.S. researcher described an as-yet-unpublished U.S. study that seems to show that phonics wins hands-down."[20]

From the time of this first announcement until a month after the publication of the National Academy of Science report (approximately fourteen months) *no one* who might have been potentially critical of the research was allowed to read a prepublication manuscript on the Foorman study. Responding to all requests for a copy, the researchers declared the study "embargoed" until publication. Although media articles were allowed to report the study's supposed findings, Foorman and her colleagues rejected all criticism as premature because the report and its actual facts had not been released. Despite all this secrecy, the researchers themselves had no qualms about including, prior to publication, their study's "facts" for the National Academy of Science committee's review of reading research and allowing these yet-unpublished "facts" to become part of a major report of a national, prestigious scientific organization. Missing from the report's description of the research findings of Foorman and her colleagues is any mention of a lack of group differences in either spelling or reading comprehension and any critical appraisal of the study, such as that presented in this chapter.

Overall, the Foorman study is remarkably deficient in substantiating the conclusions of those who conducted it. Still, considering the unqualified imprimatur the later national report gave the Foorman study, it is little wonder that the publisher of Open Court proclaimed the study the leading evidence of Open Court's effectiveness—and that many educators also believe to be so!

CLAIM

A phonemic-awareness curriculum developed in Sweden and Denmark and the subject of NICHD research grants has a body of research validating its effectiveness as an "intervention protocol" for promoting beginning reading and spelling achievement.

WHAT THE RESEARCH ACTUALLY SHOWS

☐ The commercial and professional connections of the authors of this phonemic-awareness program raise legitimate questions about these authors' objectivity when researching this and other instructional materials.

☐ When research data supposedly showing a predictive relationship between phonemic-awareness skills and later reading and writing achievement were reexamined, preschool reading achievement, not phonemic awareness, was found to be the best predictor of future reading achievement.

☐ The phonemic-awareness curriculum shows some benefits in tests on phonemic awareness and related skills, but essentially there is no scientific evidence demonstrating its effectiveness in promoting reading achievement.

☐ Articles by NICHD authors discussing the supposed effectiveness of the curriculum cite studies that appear to have been published in professional journals but, in fact, never have been.

☐ Studies on similar phonemic-awareness curricula have also failed to show a benefit for later reading achievement.

☐ Research objectivity is questionable when the authors of instructional materials are also the researchers validating those materials.

4

"Research-Based" Training Programs

The NICHD-supported reading researchers are part of a broad network of educators advocating the direct, explicit instruction of skills in beginning reading. Professional networks and connections are, of course, common, and usually the strongest associations are among people with similar views. It is expected, therefore, that researchers who believe that phonemic awareness and related skills are the chief causal influences in learning to read are most likely to read one another's papers, serve together on conference panels, quote one another, and collaborate. Although these kinds of associations can, for example, help build a body of knowledge and a career, they can also cross the line into conflicts of interest and compromised impartiality.

The Foorman study, as we have seen, appraised not simply direct code but the reading program Open Court. A coauthor of the program was Marilyn Jager Adams, a psychologist with whom Barbara Foorman has had a close working relationship—before, during, and after the study—through research on and coauthorship of a phonemic-awareness training program we will discuss in this chapter.

Ties That Bind

In 1993, Marilyn Adams translated into English a Swedish curriculum for developing phonological awareness, called the Lundberg program after its developer, Ingvar Lundberg. Immediately following the publication of this curriculum, Barbara Foorman, supported by two NICHD grants, field-tested the curriculum. During the 1993–94 school year, Foorman and her associates trained public school kindergarten teachers to use the Lundberg activities as part of their classroom curriculum. At the same time that this evaluation was under way, Foorman and the

43

publishers of Open Court were discussing using "the first-grade program [of Open Court] for empirical evaluation."[1]

In an Internet discussion of these negotiations, Adams described Foorman's "request" to use Open Court as one that "was from out of the blue. None of us anticipated it, none of us solicited it." She also described how Foorman's team "had given a bunch of kindergarten classrooms a rich program of phonemic awareness."[2] Presumably, this "rich program" Foorman was field-testing was the one Adams had translated and which would serve as the evidence for the effectiveness of the phonemic-awareness program the two would later coauthor. Given the relationship between Adams and Foorman, insistence that the latter's request "was from out of the blue" is questionable, to say the least. Regardless, permission was given and Open Court became part of the Foorman study conducted from August 1994 to May 1995.

From the end of the study through 1996, Foorman and her colleagues analyzed the data and wrote the first version of the manuscript on the research. In the fall of 1996, according to Foorman,[3] Adams and Foorman signed a contract to write a book, *Phonemic Awareness in Young Children*, coauthored with Ingvar Lundberg, that would provide a curriculum based on the Lundberg program.[4] The book, published in 1998, cited as evidence of the program's effectiveness the very research Foorman had done with the Lundberg program translated, we will remember, by Adams. In January 1997, Foorman presented the Foorman study at the conference of the American Association of the Advancement of Science. Given this history of the close professional, commercial relationship between Foorman and Adams, legitimate questions can be raised about researcher independence and objectivity.

In a comment on the publisher's decision to allow Foorman to use Open Court for research, Adams asserted that by doing so, the publisher and authors of the program "risked exposing [them]selves."[5] Given Foorman's consistent published views on the importance of direct, explicit instruction of skills in beginning reading and the insufficiencies of whole language (views consonant with those of the authors of Open Court), her professional and commercial association with one of the authors, and her ongoing NICHD-funded research on the importance of phonemic awareness, Adams' fear of exposure could be considered disingenuous.

"A Classroom Curriculum"

Introducing an article coauthored by Adams and Foorman on a phonemic-awareness-training curriculum, the editor of *American Educator*, a journal of the American Federation of Teachers, praised the curriculum as "an example of what we desperately need more of: research-based theory translated into field-tested materials that teachers could confidently use in the classroom."[6] The article itself was adapted from Adams and Foorman's book, *Phonemic Awareness in Young Children: A Classroom Curriculum*. In the remainder of this chapter, we will examine the research that teachers were asked to accept.

In a 1993 paper, Foorman and her colleagues described the Lundberg research as "longitudinal and training studies that prove a causal connection between phonological awareness and success in reading and spelling."[7] In the *American Educator* article, Adams, Foorman, and their colleagues cited research they said agreed with earlier research by Lundberg: "We, too, found that kindergartners developed the ability to analyze words into sounds significantly more quickly than kindergartners who did not have the [Lundberg] program."[8] Cited for both conclusions is a 1988 study in Denmark headed by Lundberg.[9]

This last statement is correct. Depending on how it is read, however, it can be misleading. Kindergartners "who did not have the program" were not taught with an inferior program, as the statement implies—they were given no program at all. As in the Lundberg study with Swedish kindergarten children discussed in the first chapter,[10] the "control group followed the regular preschool program, which in Denmark emphasizes social and aesthetic aspects of development and rather deliberately avoids formal cognitive and linguistic training, including early reading instruction."[11] Therefore, by the time both groups of students were tested at the end of grades one and two, the experimental group had had an extra year of reading-related instruction. It is hardly surprising, therefore, that they did better on reading and spelling tests. Without an instructional alternative, the most that might be drawn from this study is that Danish kindergarten should implement more written language–related activities. The study offers no evidence, however, for the effectiveness of phonemic-awareness training compared with other approaches to literacy learning in kindergarten.

What Causes What?

Adams, Foorman, and their colleagues go on to say, "Measures of preschool-age children's level of phonemic awareness strongly predict their future success in learning to read; this has been demonstrated not only among English students but also among Swedish" students.[12] For this claim they cite another Lundberg study with kindergartners, which reported that mastery of phonemic-awareness skills (synthesizing syllables and phonemes and segmenting words) in kindergarten predicted reading and spelling skills in the first two years of school.[13]

Contradicting this claim, however, is a later reexamination of the data by Wagner and Torgesen, which found that future reading achievement was better predicted by preschool reading achievement. These researchers concluded that "differences in the original level of reading proficiency could have been responsible for the observed relations between kindergarten phonological awareness and first-grade reading achievement, thus making ambiguous the causal implications of these data."[14]

Another study of the Lundberg program[15] conducted in Norway supposedly showed that "phonemic awareness skills strongly predict" future reading success.[16] Adams, Foorman, their colleagues, and the original investigators misapply the word *predict,* because the research only provides correlations. In this study, Norwegian first graders were tested in phonemic-awareness growth and reading achievement, but from these correlations, there is no way of knowing what caused what.

Tracking Down the Research

Foorman's field testing of the Lundberg phonemic-awareness–training program is seemingly reported in a 1997 paper appearing in the journal *Learning Disabilities* and is referred to by Adams, Foorman, and Lundberg in their *American Educator* paper as evidence for the effectiveness of the program.[17] The paper is also cited by Lyon and Moats as research helping to establish "intervention protocols."[18]

Contrary to the implication in the reference, the 1997 paper only briefly summarizes another published report, saying that the study showed that kindergartners who received "15 minutes of daily phonological awareness activities [with the Lundberg program] improved in phonological awareness skills faster than a comparison group that received the district's standard developmentally appropriate curriculum." Beyond this summary, there is no additional information: "A detailed presentation is available elsewhere," the researchers state.[19] In other words, this 1997 paper offers no firsthand scientific support for the claims of Adams, Foorman, and Lundberg and Lyon and Moats in their respective papers.

The "elsewhere" cited is a paper in which Foorman and her colleagues offer much less than a "detailed presentation"; in an eighteen-page paper on early reading intervention, only three pages are devoted to the study.[20] The article defines the training group as kindergartners in two schools eligible for participation in the Chapter 1 program (Chapter 1 children are eligible for the federal lunch program). The kindergarten control classrooms were in a neighboring school that did not qualify for the Chapter 1 program.

When demographics—gender and ethnicity—were controlled, there were no group differences in word analysis. However, when both demographics and language abilities—using a measure of expressing and understanding sentence syntax—were controlled, the researchers reported a significant difference in word analysis favoring the treatment group. Evaluating this assessment is impossible, however, because the three-page summary offers no test score information. Most important, the three pages provide no evidence that the differences in word analysis transferred to differences in reading achievement.

Because the study was reported only in two overviews of research and theory on early reading intervention and not in a journal article that might have offered adequate information, I wrote Dr. Foorman in April 1998 and asked her if the research had ever been published as a separate study. She replied that it had not been nor were there any plans to do so. There were plans for articles on two other studies, I was told, but when I inquired about them six months later, she replied, "Still working on them. We have you on our mailing list."[21]

Byrne and Fielding-Barnsley

Australian psychologists Brian Byrne and Ruth Fielding-Barnsley undertook a sequence of studies over three years aimed at validating a phonological awareness–training program that they had coauthored.[22] Cited by Adams, Foorman, and Lundberg as evidence of the effect of such training,[23] the study first reported that at the end of first grade no significant differences were found between the training and control groups in spelling regular words, irregular words, and pseudowords and in reading regular and irregular words. The training group did have one significantly superior score: they were better at reading pseudowords (*baf, jad, nel*).

At the end of second grade, the training group had statistically superior scores in reading irregular and pseudowords, but the actual differences were small. On a list of 30 irregular words, the respective average scores of the training and control groups were 24.65 and 23.73 words. On a list of 20 pseudowords, the respective scores were 17.03 and 15.57. *No* significant differences were found in reading regular words, and presumably because the researchers assumed they would duplicate the lack of significant differences in first grade, *no* spelling tests were administered. Overall, these first and second test scores do not offer especially compelling evidence on behalf of the training program.

The researchers created and administered their own comprehension test consisting of two stories and ten comprehension questions presented verbally. The training group was reported to have statistically superior scores, but because the published paper *did not* divulge the actual scores, there is no way of knowing how substantial they were.

Among the studies Adams, Foorman, and Lundberg cite, this single one reported a training effect on comprehension but simultaneously raises a number of questions. First, the comprehension test was not "blindly" administered; that is, the examiners appeared to know in which group each child belonged. This kind of knowledge is considered unscientific because it has been found to influence testing outcome and produce results more favorable to a research hypothesis than when testing is "blind." For example, the history of electroencephalogram (EEG) research on learning disabilities shows that researchers expecting to find brain dysfunctions through the use of the EEG did find many when they knew in advance which children were classified as "learning disabled"; in contrast, when the EEG analysis was blind, the EEGs of the "learning disabled" and normal learners were indistinguishable.[24]

Second, it is not clear why the researchers used a test they had devised and administered, rather than a more objective measure, such as standardized achievement tests administered by school personnel not associated with the study. Even achievement outcomes, such as the reading level of books a child was reading, the number of books read, or the child's place in a reading series, would have been relatively more objective than the comprehension test used here.

Finally, the use of investigators to validate a published training program that those same investigators authored and would like to see used in schools is not the most objective research model for appraising such a program.

"Correlations" and Training Compared with What?

"This ability to analyze words into sounds is exactly the skill that promotes successful reading in first grade," state Adams, Foorman, and Lundberg.[25] What these researchers cite in support of this idea, however, are studies that demonstrate only correlation, not causation. Also missing from these studies, aside from correlations between phonological, blending, letter-naming, and similar tests with reading test results, is a discussion of the instruction used in the classrooms—there is nothing about materials, grouping, the integration of writing and reading, and so on. Without this kind of information we cannot adequately understand the development of phonological processing abilities and reading outcomes. Moreover, Adams, Foorman, and Lundberg choose not to quote one statement from one of the papers they cite: "Recent review of the training study literature," say that paper's investigators, "indicate limited effects of phonological awareness training by itself on subsequent reading achievement."[26]

Adams, Foorman, and Lundberg refer to a study based on the use of a phonemic-awareness-training program with nonreading kindergartners. At the end of seven weeks, the skills-trained group did significantly better than the other groups on tests of word identification, indicating a beneficial influence of phonemic-awareness training on subsequent beginning reading. Once again, however, there is the problem of what the training group was compared against: one group that had minimal written language activities (letters and their sounds) and another that engaged in no written language activities. Not surprisingly, the training group had superior scores in tests matching "written symbols to the sound segments of the word."[27] The results do not demonstrate, then, that training in phonemic awareness is necessarily the written language experience that will benefit kindergartners' future reading development.

A later study led by the same reading researchers[28] used phonemic-awareness training with low-income, urban schoolchildren (approximately 85 percent qualified for "free or supported lunch") and found that the eleven-week program helped the children learn phonemic and related word skills. As in the previous study, the researchers offered the children no alternative written language experience for learning these skills. This study too was short-term, leaving unknown whether the intervention overcame the problems of other studies in applying the phonemic training to later reading success. Therefore, Adams, Foorman, and Lundberg's suggestion that these studies "clearly" show that phonemic-awareness training "significantly accelerates children's subsequent reading and writing achievement" is a considerable overstatement of the word *subsequent*.[29]

A New Zealand study that Adams and colleagues also cite to support their claim worked with children in their first few months of school. One group of children was trained in phonemic-awareness tasks, while a matching group was trained in "process writing, which is a regular feature of the whole language approach used in New Zealand schools." The phonemic-awareness group did significantly better on a task emphasizing phonemic abilities such as spelling pseudowords and a formal spelling test, but on tests evaluating the students' ability to spell in dictated sentences, to generate and write words they knew, and to identify letters, the groups showed no difference. In other words, in evaluations closer to writing actual, complex written language, a training effect was not evident.[30]

Conclusion

In response to a question I asked Barbara Foorman about the date she and Marilyn Adams signed a contract for their book on training phonemic awareness, she informed me—although I did not ask about it—that she was not accepting royalties for the book. I am not certain where the royalties will go, but direct financial benefit from the book's publication is not my concern. My concern is about interlocking research and collaboration that can create conflicts of interest, which in turn can impair objectivity. Capital in the form of professional capital can be accrued in various ways, such as through enhancing one's professional reputation, status, and influence and by obtaining research and program grants. One way of earning these kinds of professional gains is through an educational program that is highly regarded and widely used.

Given the minuscule research supporting claims about the causal benefits that phonological awareness training can have on later reading achievement, there is reason to question the empirical basis for any kind of phonological awareness–training program. Given the lack of instructional alternatives in this body of research, there is also every reason to wonder how this research could be considered evidence against the effectiveness of alternative approaches. As we have seen, Adams, Foorman, and Lundberg have yet to muster evidence, either in their own studies or the studies they cite, to support the effectiveness of their own training program, and just as much evidence exists in the other studies they cite to support the effectiveness of phonological awareness training.

CLAIM

The effectiveness of the reading program Open Court is substantiated by a body of research.

WHAT THE RESEARCH ACTUALLY SHOWS

☐ The Foorman study, the single research publication on Open Court, did not, as discussed in a previous chapter, demonstrate the program's effectiveness.

☐ In addition to the Foorman study, the publishers of Open Court have distributed only insufficiently informative magazine and newspaper articles and testimonials that praise the use of the program in schools.

5

"Coming Soon! Coming Soon!"

An article in the *Baltimore Sun* sang the praises of the success of the Open Court reading program in California. Kindergartners in "high-poverty schools" knew the alphabet and were "well on their way to reading proficiency." On the faces of first graders were "expressions that make teaching (and writing about it) worthwhile. These are kids experiencing the epiphany of reading." Perhaps it was the "Hawthorne effect," positive effects felt at being subjects in an experiment, the reporter acknowledged; nonetheless, "good things" were happening. Baltimore was especially interested in the 211 California schools using Open Court because the city had adopted the program in 1998 for its elementary schools after the program was rated "No. 1 by a national panel of reading experts convened by the *Baltimore Sun*."[1]

When I read this article, I was especially struck by the sentence "Open Court, with its heavy emphasis on phonics, has a beefy body of research to back it up." I wrote the reporter, Mike Bowler, that from my familiarity with the research I would not describe it as *beefy*. However, to ensure that my scholarship was thorough, I continued, I would like to find out about the body of work that the term *beefy* described.

Bowler replied that "perhaps [the term] was a bit hyperbolic" and that he would not again "use the word 'beefy' in a news story," but it did refer to a "body of research substantiating Open Court's effectiveness."[2] This body included a *single* study published in a professional journal—the Foorman study discussed in Chapter 3! The rest of this "research," distributed by the publisher of Open Court, consisted of anecdotal descriptions of the use of the program in two communities and some other items.

Going to the Source

SRA/McGraw-Hill is the publisher of Open Court. While writing this book, I periodically went to the Open Court section of the publisher's

Internet site looking for research information that might be posted there.[3] Month after month, over the boldly written words "Research" and "Published Articles," the same red messages appeared: "Coming soon! Coming soon!" Finally, in June 1999, one magazine article from *Forbes* by Diane Ravitch, which I will discuss shortly, appeared under "Published Articles."

The publisher of Open Court does provide a packet of materials titled "Research Related to Open Court," but here, too, the Foorman study is the only such research that has been published in a professional journal.[4] Included also is a document from the American Federation of Teachers on "promising reading programs," newspaper articles, the *Forbes* piece, and a potpourri of supportive letters and charts from several school districts. Of approximately 101 pages, about 40 are devoted to three different versions of the Foorman study.

Crown Heights

Located in the poor, predominantly African American neighborhood of Crown Heights in Brooklyn, New York, P.S. 161 began using Open Court in the late 1980s. By 1996, according to the AFT's "promising reading programs" document, 80 percent of third graders "scored above the state's minimum level, compared with 47 percent in similar schools and 79 percent in all state schools." The source of this summary is the article "The Jewel in the Crown," published in October 1997 in *Teacher Magazine*.[5]

The article itself describes the school's initial reading curriculum problem as one of "little consistency in how reading was taught from class to class, grade to grade." The article went on to say that the new principal found that "some teachers relied solely on phonics instruction, others used a whole language approach. Students moved from one teacher to another with little carry-over." The principal said he chose Open Court for reading instruction because he believed it offered a needed combination of phonics and literature. The article did not explain why he did not choose whole language, which also includes phonics teaching, as the reading program that could provide consistency.

Open Court, at least for the principal, appeared to be a middle-ground compromise between the phonics and whole language teachers that provided continuity across grades and allowed the school administration to monitor children's steps in literacy education. Nonetheless, after the program was adopted, the school's instructional program was not restricted to it alone. Whole language practices continued to constitute much of the curriculum, at least for some teachers. For instance, the school "poured thousands of dollars into supplementary reading materials." From kindergarten up, each classroom had "sets of popular storybooks, more than a hundred titles in all." These books were "an integral part of the curriculum" and teachers assigned "readings as homework, and students discuss[ed] them in class the next day." Then there was the Principal's Reading Club, which children from kindergarten up joined by going to the principal's office and, depending on a given student's grade level, reading one or more books aloud to him. On Wednesdays there was a book bazaar, where parents could buy books for their children at the cost of one dollar. In a single year, the school had sold more than 6,000 books.

A kindergarten teacher explained, "You can't just teach phonics. If there's no reason to read, they won't want to." A fourth-grade teacher used Open Court "for only about twenty minutes a day." She "like[d] to have her students do as many independent projects as possible," which included book writing throughout the year, reading novels and discussing how authors used description and developed characters, and revising and editing their stories.

How then is the influence of Open Court gleaned from such a rich texture of educational activities? We also need to keep in mind that through most of the decade during which Open Court was used in the school, the program was a version that Marilyn Adams and her coauthors had criticized and greatly revised. In an Internet discussion on a listserv open to all, Adams stated:

> Please bear in mind that the new edition of Open Court is a *TOTAL* rewrite from the 1989 and earlier copyrights. I, too, hated the voice, dynamics, literature . . . of the 1989 copyright. In fact, this was why, when originally asked by the [publishers] if I would work with them, I said no. I told them flatly that I thought the materials were wacky, ugly, no-forest-for-trees, ritualistic, sometimes even militaristic, and vintage-1950s pedagogy/classroom image and that I did not want *anybody* to think that I endorsed [the materials].[6]

Then there is the broader school setting. For principal Irwin Kurz, the key for P.S. 161's success is "high expectations." "All children can learn," he says. "It takes a village, but it's really true. It's expectations." To what extent was the emphasis on actual book reading and writing—practices inspired by whole language, not basal readers—responsible for reading achievement? To what extent was Open Court reaping credit for the extensive effort of Kurz, who worked twelve-hour days, and for the teachers' and parents' hard work? These questions cannot be answered because information about Open Court in the school is a combination of anecdote and speculation.

Poor Children and Reading Success

Writing in *Forbes* magazine, Diane Ravitch, undersecretary of education in the George Bush administration, praised P.S. 161 for using Open Court to provide "time-tested instructional methods in reading." The school's success proved that "poor children can meet the same standards as their peers" and that "good instruction can overcome social and economic disadvantage." "Not poverty," she lamented, "but bad education [was] responsible for the failure of many disadvantaged youngsters."[7] Ravitch's equation has two alternatives commonly posed in research on reading instruction for poor children, especially NICHD research. One can either reject or accept the idea that poor children can learn with the right instruction. Those who reject the notion are pessimists, disbelievers, cynics, perhaps even racists, and so forth. Those who accept it are partisans for poor children, believing in their potential to overcome extreme "social and economic disadvantage," as Ravitch puts it, and become as educationally successful as youngsters who not only do not face these disadvantages but who even have social and economic advantages beyond those of most children.

The problem with this equation is that it excludes a third alternative, namely, one that supports a comprehensive policy that eliminates the social and economic hardships these children and their families face *and* supports creating educational programs that will facilitate learning. Why, after all, should these children have to face and overcome these extreme problems? Focusing only on limited instructional bootstrap solutions while taking as a necessary evil the unjust societal class organization and distribution of wealth is a perspective that fits well within the pages of Forbes magazine and its self-ascribed characterization "capitalist tool." Unfortunately, this is also a perspective shared by many educators who care about poor children but who feel that because poverty will never be satisfactorily addressed, the most feasible policy for helping the children is a pragmatic approach that accepts the "social and economic disadvantages" and concentrates instead on improving instruction. I will say more about this in Chapter 10.

Inglewood, California

Another section on "program results" in Open Court's publisher's packet on "research" describes two schools in Inglewood, California, that have used Open Court for a number of years.[8] Excluding the publisher's half-page introduction hailing the success of Open Court, the actual evidence of this success comprises only two pages. On one, a letter from a school principal describes the racial-ethnic breakdown of the students in both the Inglewood schools involved and observes that the "Inglewood Unified School District is not doing too badly, in general. It is doing better than any minority–low income district in the state." Though presumably regarded by Open Court's publisher as a testimonial, the principal's letter does not mention Open Court even once. Instead, the principal attributes the schools' success "to at least two factors: (1) [the teachers] do a better job of teaching reading and language, (2) their kids have a longer school year because they attend intersessions throughout the year."

The second of the two pages in the "program results" section of Open Court's publisher's packet is a chart of achievement test scores in reading and language. An examination of the reading scores shown on it suggests why the Inglewood principal was reserved in her assessment of the schools' achievements. At fourth grade, the average reading-achievement ranking for the district was at the 46th percentile for both 1995 and 1996, while for one of the schools using Open Court during these years it went from the 50th percentile to the 52nd, and for the other school it went from the 55th to the 53rd. These six- and seven-percentile differences between the schools that were using Open Court and those that weren't are not to be ignored, but they hardly represent a hefty triumph for Open Court over other approaches.

Moreover, reading researcher Jeff McQuillan has compared the Inglewood school most highly praised for its success with Open Court to other California schools with similar rates of poverty and students with limited English proficiency. Using the 1998 reading-achievement scores, McQuillan showed that that Inglewood school's average fourth-grade reading achievement was comparable to that of schools with similar demographics.[9]

This is all that can be said about the Inglewood schools' "program results," because the publisher of Open Court provides no other information. Unlike P.S. 161, we do not have even the benefit of anecdotes.

Here and There

The remainder of the publisher's packet on "research related to Open Court" includes various pieces of information. There are a few achievement test results from Corpus Christi, Texas, schools in 1985–86(!). Results from a Florida school showed improvement in first- and second-grade reading scores between 1994 and 1995, following a decline in scores during 1993–94, but there is no information about what program was used prior to the implementation of Open Court or any information about the specific use of Open Court in the school. In Fargo, North Dakota, schools using Open Court are reported to have had higher achievement scores than schools using "a reading program with implicit phonics instruction," but the name of this reading program is not given. Achievement scores for schools in Shawnee Mission, Kansas, "a large suburban area," show the performance of schools that have used Open Court for one, two, and three years. The summary notes that "the demographics of these schools vary greatly both in size of the school (small and large) as well as range of socio-economic conditions." No information is provided about these variables in relation to the scores, about the program used prior to Open Court, or about the use of Open Court in the district over the three years. Finally, the publisher's packet contains some information about the Ten Schools Program in Los Angeles, California, begun in 1987. Presumably, this program had something to do with Open Court, but it is impossible to know exactly what because the words *Open Court* do not appear even once in the one-page description of the program or in the charts that compare the ten schools with others in the district.

Conclusion

About twenty-five years ago, I attended my first International Reading Association (IRA) conference. Like all IRA conferences, this one had booths of publishers' instructional materials occupying a space the size of a football field. A thorough examination of all of these materials would require several hours. Anyone attending these conferences for a decade or more has probably been struck, as I have been, by the seemingly endless array of "wonderful" reading programs. Stop and talk with the representatives of these programs, and you will hear about their successful use in this school district and that, their contribution to raising reading achievement here and there, how they have won the hearts and minds of the teachers and students who have used them—one might even hear about the research that has demonstrated their effectiveness.

No doubt most of it is true. Successes, testimonials, and even research can be found in behalf of all these commercial programs. For all the literacy problems in the United States, no matter how one tallies the problems, far more than a majority of 50 percent of children have— based on standardized test results—learned to read with programs no better, or even no worse, than Open Court. Publishers of these programs and educators who favor them do have their success stories, of course. But success stories alone are a far cry from establishing that a program can strongly contribute to ensuring that most children learn to read, that the program is superior to competing programs, that the program is successful according to certain test standards but deficient in others— or if a manufactured program is needed at all.

Also casting doubt on generalizing from success stories are two observations from the long rows of materials at IRA conventions. First, if the "successful" programs were as good as the success stories indicate, why would there be any literacy problems in the nation? After all, in the practical world of program selection over many decades, the successful programs would eventually become known and used by educators look- ing for solutions. Second, the fact that these "successful" programs are not what their success stories proclaim them to be is evident in the unending cycle of purchase, use, and rejection of instructional programs.

CLAIM

NICHD-supported research has identified a "brain glitch" that causes reading disabilities (also known as dyslexia).

WHAT THE RESEARCH ACTUALLY SHOWS

☐ The researchers never documented whether the adults used in the study were, either as children or adults, actually "reading-disabled," according to the precise definition of the term.

☐ The study obtained information about brain activity while the adults were doing simple written language tasks but did not investigate other influences on brain activity, such as emotions, motivation, or personal meanings of the tasks. Previous studies have shown that changing these kinds of influences can change brain activity when a person is doing a task.

☐ Since any two groups of normal people with different abilities to do a task will have concomitantly different brain activity while doing that task, brain activity differences themselves do not demonstrate brain dysfunctions.

6

"Brain Glitch"

"If you have a broken arm, we can see that on an X-ray. These brain activation patterns now provide us with hard evidence of a disruption in the brain regions responsible for reading—evidence for what has previously been a hidden disability." The speaker is Sally Shaywitz, the "hard evidence" referred to an NICHD study she led that reported finding a "broken arm"—a "glitch in the wiring," as she called it—in the brain of the "reading-disabled."[1] Reid Lyon praised the study because, he told the *New York Times*, it was "the first to demonstrate that there is a neurological system that undergirds all the components of reading and that a neurobiological signature underlies poor performance on reading."[2] In an interview on the *NewsHour with Jim Lehrer* on public television, Shaywitz again emphasized that "reading difficulties are real" and "have a neurobiological substrate." Lyon, in the same interview, stressed that of the studies devoted to mapping the brain pathways underpinning reading disabilities, the Shaywitz study "is more complete and show[s] what we consider the most comprehensive system" of "the neurobiological underpinning for the difficulty the kids show us."[3] These two interviews were only the more prominent among nationwide media reporting of the research.[4]

The study, part of a large body of work on the neuropsychology of reading problems, seemed to be the apogee demonstrating a repeated claim Lyon had been making about one of the "major findings from NICHD-supported research."[5] This research was demonstrating that reading problems are "associated with atypical cortical activation in neural systems that subserve language," Lyon wrote in one journal article.[6] In the Packard Foundation publication *The Future of Children*, he maintained that several NICHD investigations have linked reading disabilities to "aberrant neurophysiological processing."[7] And in the *Washington Post* he stated that NICHD-supported studies found that reading deficits were "associated with atypical functioning in specific brain areas."[8]

The Shaywitz research and a few NICHD studies are the latest of three decades of reports claiming to find a "glitch in the wiring" in the brains of so-called dyslexics, or "reading disabled." For more than two decades I have been reviewing these claims and have chronicled their continued rise and decline. The pattern begins with a spirited announcement of "breakthrough" findings of neurological dysfunctions in dyslexics, discovered through the use of technology that has become increasingly sophisticated. Often the "breakthrough" findings find their way into the media, as the Shaywitz study did, and the researchers are publicly praised for finally finding a key to the biological basis of reading disabilities. But with time—often a short time—a deterioration begins: Other researchers fail to replicate the studies. Methodological flaws are revealed. The sophisticated technology turns out to lack the diagnostic precision initially claimed for it. During the last decade, researchers have dissected dead "dyslexic" brains and reported finding cell abnormalities; radioactive isotopes used in positron emission tomography scans (PET) have supposedly found abnormal brain activity while the reading disabled read, and magnetic resonance imaging (MRI) reportedly located abnormal sizes in parts of dyslexic brains. A close examination of this work, however, soon reveals its failures.[9] Eventually, the reading disabilities field itself acknowledges the failure of such research to document its conclusions and looks ahead to the next new technologies, the next studies that will demonstrate the existence of the "glitch." In the introductory portion of the paper on the Shaywitz study, for example, the researchers appraise "previous efforts to use functional imaging methods to examine brain organizations in dyslexia" as "inconclusive."[10] Again, this kind of criticism, even from believers in the neurological basis of dyslexia, is usually heard only within the walls of the rarefied academic journal in which it appears. The criticism obviously did not strike journalists reporting on the Shaywitz findings as noteworthy, thereby prompting them to reexamine "breakthrough" research using the same technology in the recent past or to cast a skeptical eye on this new report claiming to have conclusive findings. At this point in the cycle, media do not tend to report the failure of previous research. There are no spirited denouncements, no rethinking of the long-standing theory of neurological deficits. Rather, there is only a quietude as a new "breakthrough" is spotlighted. Given the pain and continued life problems experienced by the adults nonreaders with whom I have worked—some of whom had even become suicidal because of serious learning problems psychologists had identified as due to a "neurological glitch"—this state of scientific and media irresponsibility is particularly disturbing.

The Shaywitz Study

The Shaywitz study used the functional MRI, a technology that provides information about the structure and function of the brain during an activity such as reading, with 29 "dyslexic" readers—14 men and 15 women, ages 16–54 years. Whether they actually met criteria for being dyslexic cannot be determined because, except for their IQ score range, we are told nothing else about them. Presumably, we are asked simply to suspend disbelief and accept one of two assumptions: One, regardless of the possible educational and social experiences that might be associated with the difference in brain patterns between the dyslexic and good readers—experiences such as poor instruction, childhood illness, family trauma, poor or no school attendance, insufficient nutrition, no motivation, frequent changes of schools, child abuse, emotional problems, meager preschool literacy experiences, or any combination of these—we are expected to accept that all the dyslexics shared a similar impairment in brain function. Presumably, in the study, the Shaywitz researchers consider inconsequential knowing anything about possible educational and social experiences that could have caused the reading disability because in their view one is dyslexic—a term never defined in the published research paper—due to a functional brain impairment.

Or we might be expected to accept a second assumption: There are a number of ways by which one might become dyslexic—sometimes because of impaired brain functioning, sometimes not—but these researchers had the good fortune to find 29 dyslexics all of whom happened to have impaired brain functioning that was the "neural signature" for this "impairment." If so, this was extraordinary luck for the science of reading.

We are not expected to make a third assumption, that this "neural signature" is created by the experiences of the dyslexics and/or the reading problems themselves, and that it does not represent a functional brain impairment. I propose that accepting the first two assumptions requires a suspension of disbelief greater than any scientific study should require. Furthermore, because these two assumptions are not reasonable without much, much more information than Shaywitz and colleagues provide in their research report (i.e., there is no information about the subjects and any other influence that could affect brain functioning during testing), the researchers' interpretation of the functional MRI findings is irreparably suspect.

We could, on the strength of the reasons I have outlined, dismiss the study at this point, but because of the attention given the study, more needs to be said.

An Underlying Objective of the Study

The Shaywitz study is not simply about the brain and reading. Rather, it is a study linked to the skills-emphasis theory and pedagogy, of which phonological awareness is the centerpiece, that is the hallmark of NICHD research. I shall explain how the research is crafted around this viewpoint and, unsurprisingly, how the conclusions drawn support it. Discussing the implications of the study in an interview on the Lehrer *NewsHour* television program, Shaywitz said, "this confirms what we've learned from reading tests and language tests, [that is], difficulty occurs when people with dyslexia have to try to sound out words, get to the sound structure of words."[11]

In this interview, Lyon added that the Shaywitz study helps explain what it takes to read:

> We've been able to identify that reading requires an understanding that words are made up of sound parts that will be applied to print. That's how one deciphers the code in reading. This study also shows that there is a neurobiological underpinning for the difficulty the kids show us. Their reading is slow, labored, hesitant, and primarily because they do not map these sounds well on to the print, this study indicates clearly that there are neurobiological features that explain that.[12]

At the conclusion of the interview, Shaywitz made connections among her research, phonemic skills–emphasis teaching, and NICHD research. There is a malfunctioning "neurobiological substrate" that hinders "dyslexic individuals" from learning the "sound structure of the written word," she explained. Her study "tells us where the prime difficulty is," which in turn can direct reading educators "to try to bring up that level of awareness so that children develop an understanding that words are made of sounds and that the letters represent these sounds." She concluded, "There have been some wonderful studies carried out through NICHD that have indicated already that if you use these principles, teaching children about the basic nature of language, reading really improves. It makes a real difference."[13]

My review of the NICHD research on reading has so far shown that the latter statement is not true. But let us look further at the

Shaywitz study and review its evidence and the extent to which it supports the imperative for skills-emphasis instruction.

The Tasks

The study used a sequence of five tasks. I will briefly describe them, partly because it will help illustrate the researchers' conception of *reading*.

The first task asked the subjects to decide whether lines matched (\\\V versus \V\). Obviously this required no ability with written language.

The second task asked subjects to match patterns of upper- and lowercase letters (bbBb with bbBb). This required letter, but not phonological, knowledge.

The third task asked the subjects if letters rhymed (Do *T* and *V* rhyme?). This added "a phonological processing demand," requiring knowing and comparing the sounds of the letters.

The fourth task asked the subjects if nonwords rhymed (Do *leat* and *jete* rhyme?). [Note that although the researchers used *jete* in this "nonword" task example, it is in fact an actual word, of French origin, used among English speakers and writers, a word that *does not* have a middle long /e/ or a silent /e/ ending. It describes a ballet movement of a broad leap with one leg stretched forward and the other backward, and is pronounced zhe-tay (long /a/ at the end). A possible example of too much knowledge hurting phonemic awareness.] This task required "analysis of more complex structures."

The fifth and last task required that the subjects know complex sound-symbol relationships and the meaning of words (Are corn and rice in the same category?), requiring both phonological and semantic knowledge and processing.

These attenuated tasks, while providing activities for potentially useful functional MRI information, cannot be thought to represent reading. The researchers have also contrived them around a particular conception of what they believe to be causal in beginning reading, namely, phonemic awareness. (I will return to this after discussing the details of the study.) To assume that this research can draw conclusions about reading begs the question: Would alternative definitions of reading have led to the creation of very different tasks as a means for studying brain activity?[14]

The Results

In several brain areas related to language processing, there were group differences in the pattern of the subjects' responses: the good readers showed "a systematic increase in activation" when going from the second (matching letter patterns) to the fourth task (determining if nonwords rhyme). That is, there was an increase in brain activation as the tasks increased demands for applying phonological awareness abilities. In contrast, the dyslexics showed a fairly steady level of brain activation rather than an increase in response to these tasks. Generally speaking, the brain activation for these tasks was higher for the good readers than for the dyslexics, although one area of the brain showed the reverse pattern.[15]

Examining the activation in the brain hemispheres, the researchers found that for good readers that activation was greater in the left, and for dyslexics it was greater in the right. This pattern held across all tasks.

For the researchers, these patterns suggested that "for dyslexic readers, these brain activation patterns provide evidence of an imperfectly functioning system for segmenting words into their phonological constituents." This malfunctioning was "evident" to the researchers when they asked the dyslexics to respond to increasing demands on phonological analysis. These findings, Shaywitz and her colleagues stressed, added "neurological support" to evidence obtained through studies at the behavioral and cognitive levels that pointed "to the critical role of phonological analysis and its impairment in dyslexia."[16]

Another Interpretation of These Facts

The simple fact is, the functional MRI data themselves do not carry an imprint of their meaning. Explanations can be proposed, but without any information about the *processes* through which the brain activation occurred, various reasonable explanations of the activation facts are possible, with one being as good as any other. Researchers who assume that beginning reading is primarily about making sound-symbol relationships will create research methods that contribute to manufacturing outcomes that "prove" that assumption.

Let us look at the Shaywitz researchers' explanation. Differences in activation, they assert, represent deficits that are the cause of "dyslexia," and the deficits are associated, first and foremost, with impaired phonological abilities. Failure of dyslexics in "systematically increas[ing] activation" in brain areas involved in letter-sound connections indicates that "dyslexic readers demonstrate a functional disruption" in the rear area of the brain, in which visual and sound identification and associations are made when one reads. Dyslexics have "an imperfectly functioning system for segmenting words into their phonological constituents" was the researchers final interpretation.[17]

These conclusions have little to support them because they say nothing, for example, about the personal meanings derived from the tasks or the emotions, problem-solving approaches, motivation, confidence, or learning experience of either group of readers. Studies have shown that by altering any one of these factors, patterns of brain functioning when doing tasks will also be altered.[18]

Researchers have shown, for example, that emotions are not separate from cognition, because thinking is always affective. Neuropsychological research reveals what teachers have known from their own daily work, that cognition and emotions are an intertwined "fugue."[19] Nevertheless, the Shaywitz study treats thinking as though cognition—the mental process active in the experimental tasks—were an independent phenomenon devoid of any emotional influence.

The researchers in the Shaywitz study offer insufficient information for understanding what it means that normal readers showed increased activation going from the first task to the task of nonword reading. Since there were initial ability differences between the groups, why would anyone assume that the brain activity for the two groups would be the same? In another area of the brain, when the reverse pattern was found—that is, when the dyslexics had "greater activation in response to increasing phonological decoding demands"—increased activation was said to be an instance of dyslexic deficiencies. The point is simple: unless "dyslexics" were found to have the same patterns as the normal readers—an improbability given the group differences in reading abilities—every pattern that distinguished them from the normal readers was assumed to indicate a brain problem.

A paper I coauthored on differences in brain hemisphere activation in adult beginning readers reports hemispheric changes as adults learned to read.[20] The subjects of my study did, indeed, have greater right hemisphere activation initially, when they were poor or nonreaders, but as their reading improved, their hemisphere activation changed as well toward the greater left activation pattern common to good readers. Besides the questions my study raises about causation, it suggests the deficiencies inherent in trying to understand brain activation when readers are studied at only one fixed point without any effort to make poor readers good ones.

One of the regrettable aspects of the Shaywitz research is that although the functional MRI is a potentially valuable technology for literacy studies, it is, unfortunately, rendered worthless when used to advance simplistic, reductionist conclusions. An advanced technology will never compensate for the flawed theories, methods, and data interpretations that form and inform this and similar research. Since there is more at stake here than mere scientific inquiry, and since an extraordinary technology is being used to make unwarranted claims about how children learn to read, it is the potential harm to children that is most serious.

Conclusion

Reid Lyon believes "it still may be a decade or more before scientists can confidently design a classroom curriculum based completely on neuroscience."[21] I take this to mean that he believes that eventually this will be done. The problem is, however, that the NICHD neuroscience study we have just reviewed, which portends that future, has potential classroom applications remarkably similar to those Lyon and others have been encouraging, claiming that they are based on existing scientific research. In other words, the future is now! The NICHD research on the brain and reading does not simply look at how the brain functions, it seeks to confirm foregone conclusions about the skills necessary for learning to read and the direct, explicit instruction necessary for learning these skills. Unless there is a change, future research and policy efforts connected to this research will be more of what already exists: "findings" driven by preconceived conclusions, obscurantist studies most teachers will feel ill-equipped to evaluate, and "authorities" herding teachers, children, and parents toward "scientific" findings.

CLAIM

Genes have been identified that can cause reading disabilities.

WHAT THE RESEARCH ACTUALLY SHOWS

☐ After publishing a study that reported finding high statistical correlations between genes and reading disability, the researchers wrote a "correction" letter acknowledging that several twins who should not have been part of the study had been included. After the twins were removed for a revised statistical analysis, the original correlations no longer held, and the researchers conceded that other research would be needed to confirm a connection between reading disability and genes.

☐ Additional analysis using a larger number of twins failed to replicate the original findings.

☐ Another genetics study using six families of adults who had had serious reading problems as children also failed to replicate the original findings.

☐ This family study claimed to have identified a genetic link to reading disabilities, but the statistically significant score came primarily from the correlations for one family. Half the families showed no evidence of the purported genetic linkage.

☐ Insufficient information about the actual reading abilities of the adults used in the family study prevents adequately appraising the research.

☐ Because many of the adults in the study did not seem to display a reading disability on a word-reading test, there is good reason to suspect the claim that their earlier reading problems were genetically caused.

7

A *"Broad Heritability"*

"Genetic root found for reading disorder," reported the Associated Press.[1] "Researchers pinpoint gene for dyslexia," Reuters informed its readers.[2] The *New York Times* reported: "researchers have found the approximate location of a gene that seems to be associated with dyslexia, a complex disorder that prevents millions of people from ever learning to read."[3] "Study adds evidence of genetic link to dyslexia," announced *Education Week*.[4]

These headlines of another "breakthrough" in understanding reading problems echo the claims of Reid Lyon, whose NICHD division funded the research behind the "breakthrough," and Duane Alexander, the director of the NICHD. From NICHD research, they stated, "we are learning [that] deficits in phonological processing appears, in many cases, to be heritable, as shown in family, twin, and molecular genetic studies."[5] In another overview of "major findings" from NICHD research programs, Lyon declared, "There is strong evidence for a genetic basis for reading disabilities, with deficits in phonological awareness reflecting the greatest degree of heritability."[6] And in congressional testimony, Lyon told the House of Representatives Committee on Education and the Workforce, "Our NICHD studies have taught us that the phonological differences we see in good and poor readers have a genetic basis."[7] Like the brain glitch research, this NICHD work on inherited predispositions is not solely about a connection between genes and reading but between genes and phonological awareness, the kernel of skills-emphasis theory and practice.

The Longtime Search for Bad Genes

For several decades, researchers have sought to demonstrate that reading problems can be inherited. In this search, two kinds of studies have been used, one examining patterns of reading problems within families, another targeting patterns among twins.

Early studies seeking patterns of reading problems within families found many of them. Children with reading problems tended to have parents with reading problems who themselves were the offspring of poor readers. These patterns were consistently interpreted as evidence of heritability, until researchers eventually acknowledged the inveterate problem of having no way to discern whether experience or genes produced poor reading across generations.

Studies comparing reading problems in identical and fraternal twins have had a similar problem. Researchers have assumed that the comparison would control for environmental influences because pairs of twins, whether identical or fraternal, would be treated the same and would share the same experiences. They also assumed that genetic influences would be more evident in these studies than in research on family patterns because identical twins share all the same genes, as opposed to fraternal twins, who share only half. Thus, if reading problems were found to be more common in identical pairs than in fraternal pairs, the cause, the researchers reasoned, was inherited.

The flaw in this reasoning is that identical and fraternal twins are *not* treated the same, and identical twins are more likely than fraternal twins to share similar experiences. For example, they are more likely to have the same teachers and to study together. Identical twins are more likely to be treated similarly by their parents. Studies of achievement tests and intelligence tests found that twins whose parents said they treated the pairs "exactly the same" had scores more similar than pairs not treated exactly the same.[8]

Despite these problems in twin studies, the NICHD has continued to fund them. The validity of the findings remains questionable, however, because the flawed methodology remains that of previous twin studies. Greater similarities among pairs of identical twins do not in themselves provide evidence of genetic causes of reading disabilities.[9]

The Dyslexia Gene on Chromosome 6

New techniques that allow a closer look at the genes themselves have enabled researchers to go beyond the "behavioral" level in studying the heritability of reading problems. In 1994, the prestigious journal *Science* published a paper by NICHD-funded researchers Lon Cardon and associates that claimed to have found a gene for reading disability on chromosome 6.[10] The evidence, which sparked the media headlines quoted at the beginning of this chapter, appeared especially compelling because a gene on chromosome 6 was shared to a much greater extent—an extraordinary extent—by subjects with "extreme deficits in reading performance" than by a group of poor readers with serious problems but relatively less than those with "extreme deficits." The families of the poor readers were also found to have the gene but not as frequently as were the families of the subjects with "extreme deficits." In other words, the worse the reading deficit, the findings purported, the greater the evidence of a relationship to a gene on chromosome 6. For my following discussion of the research, I have included the letter and number names of genes in parentheses for those readers who wish to compare my analysis with that in the original paper. Other readers wishing only to read my analysis at this time might want to ignore this parenthetical information.

The researchers used two groups of subjects: 114 pairs of siblings from families with a history of reading disabilities, and 50 fraternal twin pairs with at least one member of each pair having had a school history of reading problems. *Reading disabilities* are defined by these researchers as "reading performance at least two years below expected grade level and in a pattern" consistent with inheritance through a dominant gene.[11]

Some Background

In evaluating this research one must consider some genetic facts. The closer that two genes are on a chromosome, the more frequently they will be inherited together. Conversely, genes located farther apart on the same chromosome or on separate chromosomes are more likely to be passed along to offspring in random combinations. The type of research the Cardon and associates study used is called linkage analysis, which tries to determine if, among twins, siblings, or families having a common trait or characteristic, there is an association between genes on a chromosome and that trait or characteristic.

The association is explored through indirect evidence. Researchers use and "mark" known genes in a region of a chromosome and then determine the extent to which these known genes are shared by those who have a given trait or characteristic. If there is a statistically significant sharing of the marked gene, the researchers conclude that near that gene there is another gene associated with the particular trait or characteristic.

Evidence

Cardon and his colleagues presented considerable evidence of associations between reading disabilities and genetic markers, evidence that suggested a "broad heritability" of reading disability. At one marker on chromosome 6, extremely high statistical correlations were found for twins with reading disabilities, and statistically significant, although lower correlations were found for siblings (for twins the correlation was 0.0003; for siblings, 0.04).[12]

The results were even more striking when the researchers grouped the twins who had "more extreme deficits" in reading and analyzed their linkage at the same marker on a portion of chromosome 6: then the statistical correlation soared to an astronomical 0.00001! (Marker between D6S105 and TNFB: 0.00001.) When siblings with "more extreme deficits in reading" were put in one group, the correlation at this region of chromosome 6 was just short of significance (0.066).[13]

Although the study offered these compelling results, the researchers did not provide an explanation for one glaring contradiction. Siblings as a group showed a statistically significant score (0.04) for sharing the aforementioned marker (between D6S105 and TNFB), but the sibling group selected for "more extreme deficits" did not (0.066). If indeed there were an association between reading disabilities and this portion of chromosome 6, why would the sibling group with the more serious reading disabilities not demonstrate a more significant association with that portion of chromosome 6 than the sibling group with only varying degrees of reading ability? In hindsight, this inexplicable inconsistency must have presaged the "correction" that was to come.

A "Correction"

Seven months after the article appeared, the researchers wrote a letter to *Science* offering a "correction" of the results they had previously reported. Lo and behold, "reanalyses of the twin data revealed that four identical twin pairs had been inadvertently included in the [fraternal pair] sample."[14] This, it turned out, accounted for the highly statistically significant correlations. How this mistake occurred was not explained, but one can reasonably wonder how researchers with precision enough for mapping chromosomes and for performing intricate statistical analyses could have missed recognizing the inclusion of four pairs of identical twins who did not belong.

When the four pairs of identical twins were removed from the fraternal twin group, the researchers' correction letter conceded, the extraordinarily high statistical results they had obtained from the fraternal (selected) twins with "extreme deficits" in reading plunged to a level barely statistically significant (dropping from 0.00001 to 0.04). For the "unselected twins," that is, the entire group of fraternal twins used in the study—again, the criterion for the twins was that "at least one member" in each pair had a "school history of reading problems"[15]—statistical significance also declined sharply (from 0.0003 to 0.0094). In short, the "correction" letter repudiated the researchers' original conclusions: "In order to confirm evidence for a possible" linkage "for reading disability on chromosome 6," the researchers conceded, "analyses of data from additional twin pairs will be required."[16]

The changes they offered in their correction letter left unexplained one inconsistency: If genetics had been as influential as it appeared to have been in their original report, and given the criterion that at least one twin but not necessarily both have a reading problem, how did it subsequently happen that for the entire group of twins used in the study, the statistical significance of linkage on the identified region of chromosome 6 was now greater than it was for the group of twins with the worst reading problems (respective scores of 0.0094 and 0.04)? How can a group seen as having uniformly extreme reading disabilities share less of a gene on chromosome 6 than a group whose members have not only mixed degrees of reading problems but *no* reading problems at all?

The decline in statistical significance that resulted from the removal of only four of fifty twin pairs demonstrates beautifully how the weight of only a small number of heavily loaded scores can dramatically shift correlations one way or the other and cautions against placing strong confidence in a single group of subjects in this kind of genetics research. This is no small caveat because it is exactly what happened in the earlier research on chromosome 15. At first there were "breakthrough" findings linking the gene to "dyslexia," but added subjects, the researchers later found, reduced the level of statistical significance. Furthermore, a researcher using a different group of subjects failed to duplicate the original research. Eventually, the researchers of the original "breakthrough" study on this chromosome repudiated their own initial "findings."[17]

The researchers' failure to detect the misplacement of the four pairs of identical twins through the entire study illustrates that this kind of genetic-driven research does not examine alternative explanations of the causes of reading problems. Had the researchers explored the histories and experiences of the subjects—that is, what in the subjects' actual lives could have contributed to creating reading disabilities—the misplaced identical twins would likely not have been missed.

Where were the media when this "correction" appeared? Unlike with the initial researchers' "breakthrough" report, apparently no science reporter either found the researchers' error newsworthy or thought the public should know that the initial hoopla was unwarranted.

Additional Twins

After their error, the researchers added more twins to their subject pool, but in a later study of more than a hundred pairs, categorized by degrees of severity of reading problems, the findings were a long way from those of the original report. In an overview article on the researchers' work—not in a separate paper in a scientific journal—the researchers reported that in the areas of the chromosome (D6S105 and TNFB) in which very high statistically significant levels had been found, no significance was found in one of the areas (D6S105) for the entire new group with newly added twins or for those grouped by severity of reading problems (very severe or extremely severe). For the other area (TNFB), only *one* of the subgroups—the one with extremely severe reading problems—showed a statistically significant association (0.033). Overall, the addition of more twins failed to support the initially high statistical significance reported for this portion of chromosome 6.[18]

A statistically significant marker was found in one location on chromosome 6 (D6S89), but the association was not connected to severity of reading problems. That is, the group with the "extreme deficits" showed a correlation slightly less than that of the entire group of twins (those either with or without reading problems).[19] Furthermore, the group with only moderately severe reading problems had a relatively higher correlation than the one with the "extreme deficit." The hypothesis that degree of severity is associated with a marker on chromosome 6 was not demonstrated in these statistics.

A "Trait"

While focusing on the reasoning, method, and statistics in this research I have accepted the term *trait* as the investigators used it and as it is used in genetics, that is, as a quality or characteristic under genetic control, such as eye color. Whether the term can actually be used to describe reading problems is another issue, however, and begs the question: where is the evidence demonstrating that the problem has a genetic source, since no research has ever provided such proof? Cardon and associates' assumption that the reading disability they examined is a "trait" is derived in part from their declaration that they found no evidence of "significant neurological, emotional, or behavioral problems"—that is, no evidence of other factors that could explain the problem (called "exclusionary factors" in dyslexia parlance). From their research report, there is also no indication that they actually sought this evidence. Apparently thinking, as in most dyslexia research, that a simple declaration on the subject would suffice, they offer not one shred of proof that they even examined "exclusionary factors."

The researchers did formulate a quantified definition of their subjects' reading problems based on reading, academic achievement, and IQ tests, but this formula does not necessarily define a genetic trait. Countless activities and behaviors can be characterized through an aggregate of quantifiable characteristics—joke and storytelling, pie baking, tree cutting—that are not genetic traits but are instead culturally learned through formal and informal educational and work experiences, gender influences, and social contexts.

All dyslexia research efforts aimed at distinguishing the "reading disabled" from groups of poor readers have thus far proven unsuccessful. Thus, what we have in this research is an assortment of persons grouped by reading and cognitive test scores. Yet test scores themselves do not lead one to the conclusion that a common genetic trait (again, a behavior under genetic control) has been identified.

Another Genetics Study

A later study that looked for a reading-disability gene on chromosome 6 examined six families of adults who had had serious reading problems as children. The families were divided according to five measures, or "phenotypes": (1) phonological awareness, (2) phonological decoding, (3) single-word reading, (4) rapid naming automaticity, and (5) a discrepancy score between IQ and reading score.[20]

The investigators reported that an association with chromosome 6 varied for each phenotype, with it being most associated with phonological awareness and least with single-word reading. Presumably, this was a striking piece of evidence for the phonological awareness explanation of reading success and failure.

To assess the results of these studies we need to look at the results themselves and in relationship to previous studies, particularly the ones just discussed. The key findings were these:

- This study did not find significant linkage for the chromosome area (between areas D6S105 and TNFB) found in the studies discussed above. That is, this study did not replicate the chief findings of the earlier ones.

- The statistical significance for a secondary marker (D6S89) found both in the first twin group study reported in *Science*[21] and in the follow-up with a hundred twin pairs[22] was not replicated in this research.

- In the first twin study, one marker (D6S109) did not show statistically significant linkage for the twins overall, but a statistical significance was found for twins with "more extreme deficits."[23] However, the latter finding did not hold up for the hundred twin pairs as a whole or when subgrouped as having severe or very severe reading problems (reported in the *LD* article). The present study did find a significant correlation for the marker for phonological awareness (D6S109), but it was significant for only three of the families studied, with one family being the chief contributor to the statistical score. Three of the families showed *no* statistical linkage in this area.

- For another marker (D6S299), this study found a strong correlation for the phonological awareness phenotype, but the correlation was largely due to the strong contribution by one family, which made up for the lack of any such correlation for two families for phonological awareness at this or any other marker. If there is a powerful association between reading and chromosome 6, why did one-third of the six families show no consequential association at all?

The investigators of this study claimed that their results for chromosome 6 "are consistent with the results" of the previous studies I have discussed.[24] There is, however, little overlap of significant findings for any of the regions explored on chromosome 6. In fact, in contrast to the researchers' assertions, comparing the two results demonstrates that this is not a replication study!

Where Is the Deficit?

Other questions may be raised about this family study with respect to the theory of reading disabilities that underpins it and the actual reading abilities of the subjects. The investigators acknowledge that because "a number of individuals with a phonological awareness deficit— including all affected cases in the largest family (26 members)—exhibit normal single-word scores, it follows that this hypothetical gene on chromosome 6 is not itself sufficient for the full syndrome of dyslexia." In other words, although the individuals scored poorly on tests of phonological awareness, their scores on word-reading tests were those of normal readers. This discrepancy between purported cause and effect can be stated even more strongly: what is the actual impact of the supposedly genetically generated phonological awareness deficit if these adults, who had been classified as "reading disabled" in childhood, did not in adulthood have single-word reading problems? The word-recognition score is, of course, inadequate for a satisfactory picture of the reading abilities of these "affected cases," but the researchers provided no other reading profile information. Presumably, the word-reading results indicated that the subjects could read sufficiently well, therefore making unapparent a clear link among phonological deficits, markers for these deficits, and actual reading.

The question of whether a phonological awareness gene contributes to the creation of reading problems is further complicated by the fact, as the researchers themselves acknowledge, that it is phonological decoding skills, not phonological awareness, that has been identified as a "central, disproportionate deficit in dyslexia."[25] What, therefore, do the phenotype results in this research mean, if they do not jibe with the decisive skills the researchers believed were associated with reading achievement?

Back to Chromosome 15

Research claiming to find a relationship between chromosome 15 and reading disability was reported in the mid 1980s, as I discussed above, but was subsequently rejected because of methodological and replication problems. In this family research, however, a statistically significant association was found between single-word reading and one of the eleven markers examined on the chromosome. No statistically significant correlations were found, however, for phonological awareness. This finding complicated, rather than clarified, the association between genes and reading because, as the researchers themselves observed, one would think that "both single-word reading and phonological awareness would be expected to show linkage to both chromosomes."[26] If phonological awareness is associated with word reading, as it is claimed, why is there no connection between chromosome 6, where some statistically significant findings were found for phonological awareness, and chromosome 15, where only single-word reading showed any significance? No answers were offered, thereby leaving only more contradictions and questions.

Mode of Inheritance

The researchers in this family study tried without success to uncover a model of gene inheritance through either dominant or recessive genes for all the phenotypes. Some common gene markers were found among the families, but the researchers could not identify any way in which these might be inherited. Thus, "the mode of inheritance of dyslexia remains unresolved," the researchers concluded.[27] Of course it can also be posited that the mode of inheritance remains unresolved because there is none.

Reading Genes

In his book on human language, linguist Philip Lieberman critically reviewed genetic theories of learning oral language, arguing that oral language is not learned through an inherent language module or set of modules that identify aspects of language, such as syntax and phonemes. Instead, Lieberman argues, it is learned through innate brain mechanisms that include auditory perception and the associative, inferential mechanisms of the brain. In other words, associations are made from pieces of information and inferences are drawn from these associations. Children learn language by drawing inferences—abstracting "general principles"—from an array of information in varied language experiences.[28] Thus, it is the ability to draw inferences from language experiences that is critical in learning language.

Lieberman presents evidence that the basis for learning language is our neurological capacity to identify associations between things and infer general principles, rather than our having specific inherent mechanisms that grasp language structures and sound sequences and patterns. He goes on to conclude that there is no genetic "blueprint" for learning functional language or aspects of it, such as phonological awareness. Learning language shares "neuroanatomical components" involved in "other aspects of behavior." In this way, Lieberman's theory of language learning is similar to views expressed by whole language proponents:

> We comprehend the meaning of a sentence by considering the meaning of its words, the syntax of the sentence, and any other information we can bring to bear on the problem. All this takes place in a neural system that consists of circuits that link neurons in different neuroanatomical entities. These include the traditional sites of language, Broca's and Wernicke's areas, but many other parts of the brain are active when we talk or comprehend the meaning of an utterance or written text.

The "details of syntax, speech, and the words of the languages that a person knows," however, are not learned by specific genes for these details—again, they "appear to be learned by means of the associative processes that enable us to learn other complex aspects of behavior."[29]

Putting this another way, there are neural systems that include language-related portions of the brain, but the language that we learn is not determined solely by the functioning of these specific parts or by the genes for these specific parts. Learning language, spoken and written, is based on the inferential aspects of our thinking that are part of a larger neural network that includes functions and systems used for other kinds of thinking. No gene determines phonological awareness or word recognition because there is not that kind of specificity for the details of language. It is a larger thinking system that orchestrates language learning. This interpretation supports my social-psychological explanation of phonological awareness, which views any deficits in phonological awareness not as the result of a specific defect of that facet of language but as part of an absence of experiences that enable a learner to make inferences from them.[30]

In his book, Lieberman offers a caveat worth emphasizing in appraising any research about the genetics of reading problems: "We must remember that we stand on the threshold of an understanding of how brains really work. The greatest danger perhaps rests in making claims that are not supported by data or that inherently cannot be subjected to rigorous tests."[31]

CLAIM

Research by non-NICHD-supported researchers demonstrates the need for skills-emphasis instruction that the NICHD research has established.

WHAT THE RESEARCH ACTUALLY SHOWS

- ☐ Children instructed with a conventional, graded reading textbook program (a basal reading program) do show some benefits in decoding and word identification when a phonemic-awareness-training program is added to the curriculum, but the research does not demonstrate the superiority of this combination over a whole language approach.

- ☐ Children who receive phonemic awareness training by itself do not attain superior reading scores over children who receive no training.

- ☐ By demonstrating that learning phonological skills within a rich array of reading and writing activities rather than as a stand-alone program can be successful, skills-emphasis proponents actually lend some support for a whole language approach to learning.

- ☐ One group of researchers concluded that its findings "cast doubt on the simple theory that there is a direct causal path from phonological skills to reading skills."

- ☐ Non-NICHD-supported research failed to find a long-lasting reading achievement effect of phonological awareness training.

- ☐ Finding that children in a skills-training program had only slightly superior scores over those of nontrained children on a word-identification test, the researchers expressed disappointment because the differences "were rather small."

8

The "Simple" Theory

NICHD research is the leading, unified body of work justifying skills-emphasis literacy education but, as we have seen in previous chapters, it is not alone: other studies share similar assumptions, views, aims, and conclusions, which often reinforce NICHD research claims. In this chapter I will discuss a number of studies that are part of the "broad consensus" around the need for skills-emphasis education and have been cited by NICHD researchers. Ironically, some of the research shows the opposite of what skills-emphasis educators often say it demonstrates.

"Think About the Story"

Educational researcher Anne Cunningham compared "skill and drill" instruction in phonemic awareness with instruction that encouraged the conscious application of phonemic-awareness knowledge to reading. In her study, children were organized into three groups. In the "skill and drill" group, kindergartners and first graders learned phonemic segmentation and blending and similar skills but were not explicitly encouraged or taught to apply their knowledge to reading tasks. The training for the phonemic-awareness group was similar to that used in the "skill and drill" group, but "the children were directed to reflect upon their own thinking regarding phonemic awareness." Children were encouraged to try to identify unknown words through symbol-sound relationships, context, or a combination of these strategies. For example, "children were told to think about the story they were reading and decide if /b/a/t/ fits into their story of a baseball player." This made the research quite different from conventional phonemic-training studies in which "context" is verboten and phonemic training is a stepwise instructional progression that begins with small skill parts and proceeds to larger reading units.[1]

At the end of first grade these two groups were compared with a control group that only listened to stories and answered questions about them during the time the first two groups were engaged in their instructional/training programs. The group that was taught to reflect and apply knowledge was found to have significantly superior scores on a reading-achievement test, whereas the "skill and drill" group was found to have scores similar to the control group.

This study suggests that although phonemic-awareness training by itself does not produce superior reading scores over the receipt of no training, integrating phonemic training with reading and encouraging word-reading strategies that combine both decoding and comprehension can facilitate learning to read.

The study does *not,* however, demonstrate the effectiveness of the superiority of training over a whole language approach. When the children began reading instruction in first grade they were instructed with a basal reading series, a method of instruction that, as I have noted earlier, has been amply criticized as inadequate by whole language scholars. We could conclude that children in a basal reading program could benefit from a phonemic-training program as a segment of instruction emphasizing identification of words and decoding knowledge in context.

"Most Successful When Integrated"

Another phonological awareness training study with kindergarten children, by British educational researchers Fiona Brennan and Judith Ireson, was situated within the body of "recent research" suggesting that "phonological awareness is particularly influential" in beginning reading.[2]

One group of children was given explicit phonological training as part of an array of language activities that included drawing pictures and writing stories about them, writing in journals, listening to stories, and dictating stories to the teacher. A second group also learned phonological skills, but in an informal—a more implicit—way, and also performed a variety of language activities similar to those in the first group. The third group followed the "normal kindergarten program" that included writing in journals, learning letter names and sounds, and reciting rhymes but did not have a special phonological skills program.

At the end of the school year, the phonological training group did significantly better on phonological tests, but there were "no significant differences between the first two groups on the rhyme and syllable synthesis tests or on the tests of word reading and spelling." Both groups did significantly better than the "normal kindergarten" group. The researchers observed, moreover, that "the significantly superior scores achieved by the training group in this study on tasks of phonemic awareness suggest that this group should also achieve higher scores on the reading tasks, but this was not in fact the case."[3]

For Brennan and Ireson, the study meant that the assumption that phonological awareness training would lead to better reading achievement was incorrect and that phonological awareness training "is most successful when it is integrated with the teaching of reading." The researchers also suggested that the "writing experiences" of the informal learning group might have accounted for their reading success. On average, they "wrote longer stories" than either the training group or the normal kindergarten group.[4]

Overall, this study lends some support to a whole language approach insofar as it indicates that learning phonological skills within a rich array of reading and writing activities rather than as an explicit, stand-alone program can be successful. It also demonstrates that not only is there no need for a stepwise approach to literacy learning but that the stepwise approach does not work well.

"The Simple Theory"

As in the two studies just discussed, British psychologist Peter Hatcher and his colleagues compared three combinations of phonological training and reading instruction.[5] The "phonology training alone" group used a program that taught word segmentation, rhyming words, sound synthesis into words, and similar phonological tasks. The "reading with phonology" group used this program but also devoted time to reading and rereading books, writing stories, and engaging in phonological activities related to the stories. The "phonology training alone" group completed the entire program, but "the reading with phonology" group completed only approximately half of the phonological activities. A third group, a "reading alone" group, performed writing and reading activities similar to those of the second group, but the teacher omitted "any explicit reference to phonology" or letter-sound relationships.

Approximately a year after the various forms of instruction were completed, the groups were compared, and the "reading with phonology" group was found to have statistically superior test results in reading comprehension, word identification, and spelling. How do we interpret these results? The study shows that phonological training alone is not sufficient for creating the "causal" agent that phonological awareness is claimed to be. The diluted "reading alone" program simply demonstrated that teaching that forbids paying any attention to skills regardless of children's needs or requests is poor teaching. This study does raise questions about the claimed causal role of phonemic awareness in learning to read because the "phonology training alone" group "made significantly more progress in phonological skills" than the other groups, but this superiority did not translate into comparably superior literacy test scores. The authors conclude, therefore, that "phonological training alone is not a powerful way of improving children's reading skills." Moreover, they propose that their findings "cast doubt on the simple theory that there is a direct causal path from phonological skills to reading skills."[6]

Again, No Lasting Reading Benefits

Norwegian educator Alfred Lie was interested in comparing the effects on reading achievement of two kinds of training in phonological awareness, *positional analysis,* in which first graders learned the sound (phoneme) at one position in a word, and *sequential analysis,* in which sound sequences were learned.[7] These two approaches were compared to the "usual method of teaching reading in Norway," which from the scant description Lie provided, appears to be a phonics approach that teaches associations between sounds and letters, blending sounds, and so forth.

Although the sequential analysis group had the highest reading scores at the end of the school year, by the end of second grade, the three groups were reading at essentially the same level. On the other hand, the training groups had significantly better scores in spelling in both grades than did the group taught by the "usual Norwegian method."

We see here a failed attempt to find a long-lasting reading-achievement effect of phonological training. Whatever the short-term benefit in reading or longer-term benefit in spelling, the most that can be said here is that children learning to spell through the Norwegian beginning literacy instruction, which seems heavily based on phonics, could benefit from the training programs employed in this study.

"Disappointing Results"

Other training research was done in Germany by psychologist Wolfgang Schneider and his colleagues. In the first of two studies, kindergartners used a German version of the Lundberg program (discussed in Chapter 4). As in other training studies, the "long-term training effects of phonological awareness yielded disappointing results" because at end of the first and second grades, no significant group differences were found on reading and spelling tests.[8]

Perplexed by the results, Schneider and his colleagues looked at how the teachers conducted the training program and found that some had taught it "consistently and perfectly" while others had not. At the end of first grade, the "consistently trained" group "performed better" on the reading and spelling tests than did the inconsistently trained children and a control group that received no training. These results were not sustained, however, to the end of second grade, when not only were no statistical differences found, but the "control children tended to outperform the two training groups on the reading test," although the differences were not statistically significant.[9]

Perplexed again by the failure to achieve the long-term training effects they had anticipated, the researchers decided to do another study, ensuring this time more thorough and consistent teaching. One difference in the assessment was the use of a revised version of the reading test, which turned out to be more difficult than the original one and inappropriate for assessing the children. As a result, this study, unlike the first, had no measure of reading comprehension. On a reading test requiring word identification, the training group had better scores, but the researchers were nonetheless disappointed because "the effect sizes" on the tests "were rather small." For example, on a reading test of 140 words, the training group identified an average of 82.22 and the control group identified 76.99.[10]

The study was also marred by the loss of two classrooms "because the school principal and the classroom teachers did not want to cooperate in the project."[11] The researchers did not explain why the project was rejected. Putting this rejection together with the group of teachers who did not follow through on the training program in the first study, however, could raise the possibility that a significant portion of kindergarten teachers did not feel the program would be helpful to their students. The rejection, at the least, raises a serious question about teachers' perception of the usefulness of the Lundberg program.

Ninety-Minute Triumph

Also cited as part of the evidence of the causal linkage from phonological ability to reading achievement are publications that deserve only brief comments. One of these describes a "training program" that ran from three to four days for a total per-child time of approximately 90 to 135 minutes.[12] During this time, reading-disabled second- and third-grade children were taught "phonemic discrimination," that is, to distinguish between phonemic consonant-vowel combinations such as /bi/ and /di/. Upon retaking a phonemic-segmentation test (for example, "Say bug without the /b/ sound") that had been administered before training, the trained students had superior scores and showed greater improvement in test scores than those of untrained reading-disabled students. The test required no reading, and no attempt was made to see if the training effects carried over to actual reading. The research design of this brief study, in other words, had no "linkage" between the skills and reading, making impossible any conclusion about causation.

A Cause Without Causes

British psychologist Peter Bryant and his colleagues found that children's phonological abilities at about four years of age were strongly correlated to their reading and spelling achievement at the end of first grade. This connection appears to support the claim about the causal role of phonological abilities, until we begin to ask questions about causation, such as: Where do the phonological abilities come from at four years of age? Do they come from experience and informal education within the family? It does not seem so, conclude the researchers, after examining "mother's education." Could phonological abilities have developed as part of children's overall language abilities, such as vocabulary and expressive language? No, say the researchers, because a statistical analysis found that phonological abilities "cannot be explained away as a mere symptom of a more general linguistic ability."[13] Were phonological abilities linked to the children's age at testing? To intelligence? Neither of these explained the differences, say the researchers. What about instruction? Again, no connections, say the researchers.

Especially relevant to proponents of skills-emphasis teaching should be the question: Why did instruction appear to do nothing to change the effect of early phonological abilities? We cannot even begin, once again, to answer the question because we are provided no information about the kindergarten curriculum and only know that reading instruction in first grade was "a mixture of 'phonics' and 'whole word'" (not to be confused with whole language).[14]

Overall, the study by Bryant and his colleagues offers little understanding about causal connections and provides no information about what might have "caused" the array of phonological abilities among the children at age four. Should we be satisfied with a lack of explanation for these causes? Did phonological awareness emerge at age four as if by magic? As I shall discuss in the next chapter, this study's non-explanation runs counter to more probing studies that provide evidence of the contribution of social background in learning phonological skills.

Conclusion

From these studies and others frequently cited on behalf of skills-emphasis literacy instruction,[15] several conclusions can be drawn. First, almost all the studies show no long-term training effects on reading achievement. Where effect has been shown, it has been "small" and temporary. A number of studies have shown short-term effects of training programs, but because they do not extend beyond kindergarten or first grade and do not include more than rudimentary reading tasks, given the results of the studies on longer-term effects that I have reviewed, nothing will be gained in reviewing them.[16] Second, none of these studies involves whole language, even though arguments that draw policy conclusions use this research as a battering ram against whole language. Even if every study discussed showed a long-term training effect on reading achievement, none of it would be evidence against whole language teaching. Third, some studies do suggest that traditional teaching with basal reading series or a phonics curriculum might benefit to some degree from a phonological training program. However, the premise of this expectation shares common ground with whole language in its criticism of the inadequacies both of basals and phonics-emphasis curricula. Fourth, from the early research on the "causal" influence of phonological awareness, researchers have moved toward recognizing that phonological abilities are learned best when they are related to reading and writing activities rather than as a singular skill. This shift has moved the phonological awareness paradigm closer to rather than away from whole language theory and practice.

CLAIM

As if by magic, many children acquire phonological awareness and rudimentary literacy abilities prior to beginning schooling. Those children who have not attained these abilities at that time require direct, systematic instruction in reading and writing skills.

WHAT THE RESEARCH ACTUALLY SHOWS

☐ Social class experiences have a major impact on the development of children's written language abilities.

☐ Most children from middle-income families—where there is more likely to be a rich written language environment than there is in lower-income families—acquire greater knowledge of phonemic awareness, letter names, vocabulary, written language syntax, and simple words, etc., than do children from lower-income families.

☐ The growth of literacy competence through immersion in these rich written language environments is not due to any "training" in essential skills.

☐ Literacy outcomes associated with social class experiences reveal the need to provide rich written language experiences for all children and to ensure high-quality economic and social conditions for their families.

☐ Phonological awareness, although important in early literacy development, needs to be seen as a "marker" of access to extensive literacy opportunities.

9

Magic Markers

Despite disagreements over the necessity of direct, explicit skills instruction, there is at least agreement that not all children need it because so many learn to read without it. Testifying in support of the Reading Excellence Act before a House of Representatives committee, Reid Lyon stated:

> Some children learn to read and write with ease . . . Even before they enter school, they have developed an understanding that the letters on a page can be sounded out to make words and some preschool children can even read words correctly that they have never seen before and comprehend what they have read. Research has shown that some of the children, before school, and without any great effort or pressure on the part of their parents, pick up books, pencils, and they are on their way, *almost as though by magic.*[1]

What is the "magic" of which some children avail themselves? Do these children, one fine day, simply master beginning reading without assistance from adults in their families or the preschools they attend? Just as children seem to learn to speak "by magic," does the reading ability of "some" expand miraculously with each passing week?

From the head of the NICHD division that claims to be dedicated to the scientific study of reading, the statement is particularly peculiar. It gives the impression that this blossoming cannot or need not be explained by evidence and additional examination, when in fact there is a considerable body of evidence explaining the preschool influences on reading progress that might seem magical to Lyon and others. In this chapter we will look at that evidence and what it reveals about how phonemic and related skills can be learned.

Class Magic

Marilyn Adams, Barbara Foorman, and their colleagues have observed that "research indicates that, without direct instructional support, phonemic awareness eludes roughly 25 percent of middle-class first graders and substantially more of those who come from less literacy-rich backgrounds. Without these skills, the children have serious difficulty in learning to read and write."[2]

Leaving aside the question about whether this percentage is even accurate, the main point of this statement by Adams and her colleagues does accord with the generally held view among reading researchers that the overwhelming majority of middle-class children have phonological skills when they enter school and do not require skills training to acquire them. Transposing the researchers' findings, we can say that approximately 75 percent of middle-class first graders acquire phonemic awareness through their "literacy-rich backgrounds." Children's literacy abilities when they enter school might seem to have been attained "almost as though by magic," but the "magic" has largely to do with the good fortune of learning written language within families able to promote "literacy-rich" experiences.

Running through the research reviewed in this book is a recognition that social class experiences influence how and the extent to which children learn reading skills. One example is the decision of one group of NICHD researchers "to work with children who attend inner-city schools." Their reasons: First, "for experimental reasons, to reduce the likelihood that the participants would enter the project with either advanced phonemic awareness or reading skills." The second reason, which expressed the best of intentions commonly stated in phonological awareness investigations, was to find "effective intervention strategies" for this "at-risk population."[3] Whether or not this kind of research is the best way to help this "population" I will discuss later. For now I simply want to emphasize that this body of research recognized the strong association between social class experiences and reading-skills attainment.

Lyon himself, looking behind the magical veil, noted that "children who have stimulating literacy experiences from birth onward" are most likely to learn to read in school because they have "an edge in vocabulary development," understand "the goals of reading," are aware of "print and literacy concepts," and have been engaged in the "language play that develops an awareness of sound structure and language patterns." Conversely, "children raised in poverty," from homes "where the parents' reading levels and practices are low," or where proficiency in English is limited, are less likely to have had these experiences before entering kindergarten or first grade.[4]

Class Studies

More than two decades ago, researchers from Duke University concerned about the low reading achievement of many poor children examined the proposition "that a major cause for poor children's frequent difficulties in learning to read may be that such children tend to have serious problems with phonemic analysis." Testing kindergartners from low-income families (occupations included factory worker, construction worker, poor farmer, and waitress) and middle-class families (occupations such as doctor, lawyer, college teacher, and businessperson), they found that "most of the middle-class children scored at or near the maximum possible" on phonemic-awareness tests, "while most of the disadvantaged children earned low scores." There were no "race differences within social class"—the prevailing influence was class.[5]

A study by Australian psychologist Judith Bowey looked at the phonological abilities of five-year-old children from middle-class and lower-class families, defined by a classification scale of occupations. Bowey undertook the study partly because "relative to the enormous literature on socioeconomic status differences in language development, there has been little research investigating the development of phonological abilities as a function of parental" socioeconomic status.[6] To minimize social class overlap, children from extreme social class groups were used in the analysis. In measures of vocabulary, various phonological awareness tasks, and letter-name knowledge, Bowey found that children from the higher social class did markedly better and continued to do so as they learned to read in first grade.

A more in-depth study by psychologist Christopher Lonigan and his colleagues compared preschoolers from middle- to upper-income and low-income families, determined by eligibility for state-subsidized child care. The majority of children in the first group were white (93 percent) and in the second group, African American (82 percent).[7]

The children were administered four tasks of phonological awareness: rhyme oddity (*fish, dish, book*); alliteration oddity (*toad, toaster, girl*); blending words, syllables, and phonemes; and elision of portions of words (remove *bat* from *batman*). On all tasks, children from the middle-income homes performed significantly better than those from the lower-income homes. By age five, the middle-income children did dramatically better on the blending tasks, thereby demonstrating their proficiency in a skill considered to be strongly related to learning to read. Respective test scores for blending words were 93.8 versus 26.7; for blending syllables, 89.2 versus 13.3; and for blending phonemes, 80.0 versus 6.7.

All but one of the middle-income children knew at least some letter names compared with 62 percent of the lower-income children. Thirty-eight percent of the middle-income children could read at least one word, but *none* of the lower-income children could read any.

Why These Social Class Differences?

What is it that creates the substantial social class differences in the "phonological sensitivity" for very young children? Lonigan and his colleagues proposed that phonological awareness might come from the "cumulative effects, or changing quality, of their home literacy, reading, or language environments." They cite the "large literature" that has "documented differences in book ownership, shared-reading frequency, and other potentially instructional activities between higher and lower social class groups." The researchers conclude that children are most likely to learn phonological awareness and other reading abilities within a rich written language environment.[8]

This is an interpretation with which Marilyn Adams would be likely to agree. Posing the rhetorical question "Where do prereading skills come from?" she answers, "Early experience with print." "One irrepressible interpretation" of the extent of a child's reading success in first grade is that it "depends most of all on how much she or he has already learned about reading before getting there." This interpretation, Adams states, "seems soberingly correct."[9]

Using her four-year-old son as an example, Adams proposes that if he "or almost any of his middle-class preschool peers were given a prereader test," they "would probably do quite well" on tests of rudimentary phonemic awareness, such as blending and syllable splitting, and letter naming. Although he probably would not be able to read any words, nonetheless, Adams believes that when he "eventually receives formal reading instruction, he will do fine." Why? Not because of "his letter recognition skills and phonemic awareness." These skills, Adams concedes, are "in some sense just tips—albeit critical and diagnostic tips—of a reading readiness iceberg."[10]

Studies have found that more than phonological awareness is learned in preschool literacy experiences. Storybook reading, for example, helps children experience language's characteristics and structures. Pretend reading mimics storybook intonation patterns. Storybook reading can make children aware that written language is symbolic of actions, people, things, and so on, and that, unlike spoken language, it is independent of context—that is, it is not like everyday spoken language that is related to situations and people. Reading frequently to children helps teach them to use participles (verbs used syntactically as adjectives); attributive adjectives (for example, "The blue house" instead of "The house is blue"); and adverbial clauses (-ly adverbs to modify verbs: "She quickly followed the parade"). This interactive array of abilities is part of the preschool literacy growth that contributes to literacy.[11]

Tom Nicholson, a New Zealand educator who has done extensive research on phonemic awareness, addresses the influence of social class in an essay on "closing the gap on reading failure."[12] Nicholson draws upon several studies to outline key social class differences that contribute to reading outcomes. Children who learn to read before they enter school, he argues, were read to daily, played with literacy materials such as magnetic letters and alphabet blocks, used ABC books, played sound games, used their literacy knowledge to make words with plastic letters or blocks, and so forth. These experiences and materials were generally provided because of the extensive time and resources parents put into their children's learning.

Explaining social class differences, Nicholson supports earlier explanations: "In contrast to the experience of children of middle-class parents, children in low-income families may have had very different early literacy experiences." One study Nicholson cites found that preschoolers from low-income families rather than engaging in daily storybook reading were read to an average of only five times a year. The majority of poor children did not own a single book, while more affluent children owned an average of fifty-four. Preschoolers categorized in another study as "either 100-book kids or 1,000-book kids"—the latter were read to at least daily from the time of their first birthday—had dramatic group differences in literacy development. A survey of home environment that Nicholson himself conducted found that poorer families were "unable to provide the print-related experiences that can be found in many middle-class families" for reasons "probably economic."[13]

A New Zealand study undertaken for teacher training "showed that although children from low-income backgrounds *can* be successful in school, the odds are very much against them." Their families are more likely to be under financial and social stress and "less able to provide the kind of support available in middle-class homes." Additionally, when children have academic trouble in school, low-income parents, because of their low-status jobs and lesser education, are less likely to feel confident approaching the school.[14]

Similar analyses can be found in the media. An article that was part of the "Reading By 9" series in the *Los Angeles Times* addressed the "poverty factor" in learning to read. Describing the educational and social plight of a young boy, Ruben, and his family, the reporter wrote, "He is among the thousands of third graders in the Los Angeles region who cannot read at grade level and are in danger of falling hopelessly behind in school. And like many of those children, he is poor." From 1991 to 1996, "the number of children living in poverty in Los Angeles County doubled to about 651,000," approximately 33 percent of "all school-age children in the county." Given the "powerful impact" of poverty on academic achievement, it is not surprising that "the 100 worst-performing schools" in the district "were clustered in the poorest neighborhoods." The harsh conditions of poverty—such as excessive work, excessive hours, insufficient income, no medical insurance, and substandard housing—hinder low-income parents from devoting adequate time and energy to their children's literacy experience and from being able to allocate funds for literacy materials. Affluence had a different impact, one school official observed: "We were always very successful academically when our kids were coming from middle-class families."

Ruben attended a school in "one of the most densely populated and economically disadvantaged areas in the state. About 86 percent of the school's third graders could not read at grade level." Although tutoring could have made a difference, the school's "only tutoring program for struggling readers serves about a dozen first-graders a year." A second-grade teacher at the school who wanted to start an after-school remedial reading program first had to "win a modest $2,500 grant from the district."[15]

Ignoring the Obvious

After identifying social class differences in literacy outcomes, one research group anguished that "the reading achievement of large numbers of children from economically disadvantaged homes is so low as to have caused widespread concern." But the central problem, they explained, might be, as "some experimenters have proposed, that poor children starting school may lack the ability that middle-class children possess to hear the differences between phonemes." One might deduce from this explanation that Wallach believes that all the literacy experiences and advantages of middle-class children are only important to the extent that they facilitate phonemic awareness: "It seems likely that lack of phonemic awareness skills plays a significant role in poor children's frequent difficulties in learning to read. Since it has been demonstrated that these skills can be successfully taught, doing so for children who lack them when starting school seems indicated."[16]

Adams, after reviewing research on the impact of social class on reading achievement and describing the extensive nurturing of her son's literacy growth, exhorted that "we have not a classroom moment to waste" on behalf of poor children and offered this recommendation: "The great value of research on prereaders may lie in the clues it gives us toward determining what the less prepared prereader needs most to learn. The evidence strongly suggests that we must help them to develop their aware-ness of the phonetic composition of words. And we must also teach them the letters of the alphabet and the phonetic significance of each."[17] Presumably following mastery of Adams' preparation, poor children will then be on a more than adequate footing for future reading success.

After their detailed analysis of "significant social class differences in growth in phonological sensitivity," Lonigan and his colleagues rec-ommended that the course "likely to be most productive during the preschool years" is "screening of children for phonological sensitivity" that would "predict the children's later reading achievement."[18]

Drawing similar conclusions, Bowey, after documenting "socio-economic status differences in preschool phonological sensitivity and first-grade reading achievement," proposed that "schools in low socio-economic status neighborhoods" should "include activities that foster children's understanding that words can share sound patterns and, per-haps later, activities that demonstrate that words that look similar share similar sounds."[19] As in the recommendations in the other studies I have quoted, here too is no discussion that hints at the need for even moderate social and educational changes that could provide children of low-income families the same experiences and benefits available to children from higher-income families.

Nicholson, too, after detailing the social class "gap" between read-ing success and failure, proposes closing that gap with the familiar "phonemic awareness skills": within all that middle-class parents facili-tate for their children's literacy development, facilitating phonological awareness skills and letter-sound relationships is the crucial element "less likely to happen in low-income families," he maintains. Reviewing some of the training studies I have discussed in the preceding chapters—but arguing for their effectiveness—Nicholson counsels "that phonemic awareness and simple phonics instruction could help to bridge the gap between pupils from different socioeconomic backgrounds."[20]

One wonders if skills-emphasis researchers, all of whom are like-ly to be part of the professional stratum of the middle class, would apply their recommendations to their own children. Would they reduce to a fraction all they would normally devote to promoting their children's literacy, assured that most of that array of literacy resources and experiences would be extraneous to the factors that are the actual strong determinants of literacy success? As researchers, having distilled beginning reading's central determinants, would they give their children only the causal factors they recommend for poor children—training in phonemic skills?

Not Touching the Untouchable

These studies and discussions on connections among social class, phonological awareness, and reading achievement miss the lessons to be drawn from the very information they provided. The more the beginning reading knowledge—including greater phonemic-awareness knowledge—available to children from middle-income families is obtained through engagement in a variety of written language experiences, the more likely those children will learn to read and write. This knowledge develops through the mentoring, the materials, and all the opportunities for individual literacy activities and preschool educational programs that parents are able to provide. There is no investigation of preschool literacy competence that has found that parents who nurture this competence do so by providing "training" in essential skills. Certainly numerous instances of activities that promote skills are likely to go on, such as rhyming games, playful exchanges that substitute sounds in words, children writing and making connections—and getting help making connections—between letters and sounds, adults pointing to letters in a storybook and asking children what sounds they make. This learning of the "alphabetic principle," however, is always part of a larger whole that encourages children's learning. Most parents who have nurtured their children's early literacy have never heard of phonological awareness. They are likely to know from engaging and encouraging their children in literacy activities that children, through both parental mentoring and their own inferences, derive an understanding that spoken sounds can be separated from one another, can be associated with letters, and letters with sounds.

The early literacy successes identified in the social class research reveal the need to go beyond literacy experiences and instruction, especially as narrowly defined in phonetic training, and address the importance of adequate overall conditions for families and children. Poverty means that adults are less likely to have sufficient time or materials for nurturing early literacy and children are less likely to have adequate nutrition, health, housing, clothing, and other life basics that nurture learning. Of course middle-income attainment is likely to be accompanied by higher parental education, which facilitates encouraging early literacy. However, if low-income parents were to have adequate income for high-quality preschool programs—and if high-quality preschool became a national priority—these programs could compensate in varying degrees for educational shortcomings low-income parents might have in helping their children.

Conclusion

The social class research indicates that phonological awareness is a causal influence in early literacy growth, but only one among many. Moreover—and more important—phonological awareness needs to be seen as a "marker" of access to extensive literacy opportunities and activities. It is a marker of adult-supported social and literacy experiences that promote literacy achievement. If phonological awareness is not seen as a marker first and a causal agent second, the full significance of it will be misinterpreted and the potentially valuable research on social class and phonological awareness will be misapplied in social policy. Seeing phonological awareness as a chief causal agent leads to the misdirected and inadequate question: What kind of training programs and specific experiences are required to teach phonological awareness? Seeing phonological awareness as a marker, however, allows the more promising question: How can all children obtain the comprehensive written language experiences that will ensure continued literacy achievement? Educational policy should strive to duplicate the written language conditions and experiences that produce the predominant literacy success including literacy "skills" successes indicated in these social class studies.

CLAIM

Scientific evidence demonstrates the need for direct, explicit instruction of "alphabetic code" skills in beginning reading and the likelihood that this kind of instruction is the most powerful weapon for promoting literacy.

WHAT THE RESEARCH ACTUALLY SHOWS

☐ Far from being neutral and objective, most of the studies contain an a priori conclusion about the causal effects of skills-emphasis literacy teaching, a conclusion that has helped induce numerous methodological defects and has bent the research data to it.

☐ The research excludes consideration of numerous facets of children's lives that vitally influence their literacy achievement.

☐ The research reinforces acceptance of the mistaken, narrow view that limited instructional measures can be sufficient to ensure the literacy success for all children, and concomitantly, reinforces rejection of the need to create broad social policy initiatives that would include but go beyond instruction to ensure children's literacy success.

10

Science and Children's Learning

Let us now consider again the claim that scientific evidence demonstrates the need for the direct, explicit instruction of skills in beginning reading, for school policy, and for state and federal legislation mandating this instruction. Having reviewed the major evidence for this claim, let us again ask whether it is true that "one of the most well established conclusions in all of behavioral science [is] that direct instruction in alphabetic code facilitates early reading acquisition."[1] Is Reid Lyon correct in describing "the NICHD supported research" as "distinctive" in "its methodological rigor"?[2] Is NICHD researcher Benita Blachman accurate in announcing the "good news" that "there have been scientific breakthroughs in our knowledge about the development of literacy" and "what we know from research" is that "direct, systematic instruction about the alphabetic code . . . might be the most powerful weapon in the fight against illiteracy"?[3] Are legislators who mandate replacing whole language with the direct, explicit teaching of sound-symbol connections to be praised for relying on "research issues to guide policy"?[4] A close examination of the research presented here yields a decided answer of "no" to all of these questions.

The "Studies Have Taught Us"

Lyon commonly describes the findings of the NICHD research this way: "Our NICHD studies have taught us" or "our studies have helped us understand." These descriptions, used whether giving formal testimony at a U.S. House of Representatives hearing on reading legislation or writing informally for a general audience in a newspaper column,[5] cast the research as a process impartially created by researchers, resulting in data impartially inspected and interpreted.

Contrary to this depiction, we have seen that NICHD and similar studies have "taught us" that this research carries the vivid imprint of numerous a priori decisions and interpretations that inevitably shape the results of and claims about the research and produce bad science. Among the many defects in the research we have reviewed are the

- use of particular explanations (theories) of learning to read that lead researchers to ask certain questions and omit others that might have offered more illumination;
- confusion of correlation with causation by not examining what might cause a purported "cause";
- confusion of information with explanation;
- transformation of insufficient data into "meaningful" conclusions;
- rare use of meaningful control comparison groups to compare how phonemic and related skills could be learned in ways other than by direct, explicit instruction;
- narrow focus on instruction and the disregard for all else inside and outside schools that influences teaching and learning outcomes;
- lack of exploration of the regular instruction children received that the researchers thought required a supplementary training program in skills;
- lack of exploration of the regular reading instruction that might have affected correlations between preschool levels of phonological awareness and subsequent reading achievement;
- failure to explore why early preschool phonemic skills should have a strong effect on later reading outcomes and why regular instruction seemed helpless in changing these outcomes;
- use of methodologies that compared preschool training programs to no programs at all;
- failure to consider that within the research itself is evidence that phonemic awareness is a marker of children's written language experiences and one causal agent among many; and
- frequent use of measures that insufficiently represented "reading."

Although the list could be longer, it is sufficient to demonstrate that what this research has "taught us" has largely been a function of what its researchers wanted to teach and that it was conducted around the lessons to be taught. The research reveals an obsession with formulating all data into a demonstration of the causal effects of the "alphabetic principle." Another obsession is its determination to find, all facts to the contrary, a positive connection between training programs and literacy outcomes. The researchers never ask what else is going on in schools, classrooms, children's lives, the children's minds, and social policy that produced the reading problems in the first place.

Dismissing Alternative Instruction

The severe limitation of this direct-instruction research would perhaps be harmless if it were simply aimed at making direct instruction of skills more effective. It is harmful to children's learning, however, because it reinforces the use of a form of instruction that—while proficient at teaching phonemic skills, according to its very research—shows no more than its proficiency in teaching phonemic skills, not in reading; has not been shown to be more effective than other kinds of instruction; limits the ability of teachers to select other forms of instruction, regardless of their merit; and reinforces a top-down, managerial schoolwide, statewide, and—if those promoting federal legislation get their way—nationwide, singular approach to literacy learning.

None of the concerns about the distortions in understanding how children learn to read, the failure to consider the multiple influences on reading achievement, or the misrepresentation of the actual findings of studies would matter as much were they not part of a nationwide attack on other literacy approaches and research. More than an attack, this body of research is part of a full-scale effort to extinguish whole language from the schools and to discredit its research and theory.

Exclusion of Important Influences on Literacy Achievement

This skills-emphasis research is also bad science because it reinforces a narrow view of what needs to be and need not be studied to ensure children's literacy success. A good example of this is Barbara Foorman's explanation that the purpose of her research—and, by implication, the NICHD research—is to address "the broader question of under what conditions and for what types of children do certain types of reading instructional methods work, and for how long."[6] This description of the purposes of the NICHD research can be found in most of Lyon's work that I have cited throughout this book. For the "Foorman study," this meant looking at mostly poor "types of children" and comparing several "types" of instruction. In her study, as in most of the research we have reviewed, the only "conditions" are those closely—and narrowly—related to instruction. It is research with a methodology based on acceptance of all the "givens" of poverty and looking to see how instruction, by itself, can help make these poor children literate.

The research, as Foorman describes it, also hopes to "allow [these poor children] to overcome the burden introduced by the lack of equity apparent in many aspects of our society."[7] In other words, the "conditions" guiding the NICHD research are confined to those of instruction and do not, as conceived in the research, include attention to what this "burden" is that children bear and how the "burden" affects their learning. Something as minimal and basic, for example, as "How does a hungry child learn?" casts no shadow on the single-minded track on which this research moves.

This kind of research fits perfectly within, for example, the political givens for the poor of Texas under Gov. George W. Bush, whose Reading Initiative for the state is grounded in the view of reading offered by Foorman, Lyon, and the NICHD studies.[8] Reading Initiative documents refer repeatedly to NICHD studies and other research reviewed in this book. Foorman, Lyon, and other NICHD researchers have participated in conferences promoting the Reading Initiative. In 1997, Foorman received a half-million-dollar grant from the Texas Education Agency to develop a reading diagnostic test. In mentioning these associations, I am not implying that there is any kind of formal or informal connection and design between Bush and Foorman and her colleagues at their Center for Academic and Reading Skills at the University of Texas–Houston. Rather, I am proposing that both approaches to what counts as conditions for promoting literacy are similar, with reading studies disregarding certain conditions by omission, and the governor, with greater power over policy, doing so by commission.

The Texas Reading Initiative, and its proclaimed goal of making every child in Texas public schools a reader, is near the top of Bush's policy list. To this end, the governor has pushed for "a rigorous core reading curriculum that is knowledge-based, back to basics and phonics-driven" while remaining less concerned with other areas of children's lives. At the same time that Bush is supporting research of what he believes aims at the educational uplifting of poor children, Texas remains fiftieth in per-capita government spending on social programs and "fifth in the percentage of people living in poverty." While giving tax breaks to oil well owners, Bush has presided over a state that is thirty-eighth in teachers salaries and forty-seventh in the delivery of social services. The governor has fought to "hold the line on health insurance for children whose families earn too much to qualify for Medicaid but too little to purchase private health insurance," a policy that has affected "1.4 million children in Texas who have no health insurance."[9]

Within such a political structure, literacy research and practice that focus so primarily and so narrowly on instruction reinforce the indifference of policy makers toward many areas of the lives of children and their families that are critical in learning. Many researchers whose work I have reviewed no doubt are disturbed by poverty and perhaps they concentrate on instruction because they feel that although they are not able to influence political policy, they can at least make educational changes that will help needy children. Biologists Richard Levins and Richard Lewontin argue that "in Western ideology 'pragmatic' is a term of praise, in contrast to 'ideological,' which is pejorative. For scientists, pragmatism means accepting the boundary conditions" of the society. "It means getting on with the job" and putting aside concerns about the "injustice of social arrangements." Concerns for injustice are often considered "ideological," in contrast to "scholarly cool."[10] Additionally, many reading researchers feel that focus on reading instruction is the proper professional focus. Regardless of intentions, this narrow line of approach to research serves to reinforce existing politics and policy that fail to address societal inequities that are inseparable from how children learn.

The criticisms I level at the limitations of this research methodology do not mean I am urging everything to be studied at the same time. I am, however, criticizing the deficiencies in this approach because it limits what is "science" and *never* gets to the myriad influences and processes that constitute learning. Sociologist C. Wright Mills observed that the social scientist who spends "intellectual force on the details of small-scale milieu" is "not putting his [or her] work outside the political conflicts and forces of" the time. That scientist is "at least indirectly and in effect 'accepting' the framework" of society. "But no one who accepts the full intellectual tasks of social science can merely assume that structure." Mills insists, in fact, it is the scientist's "job to make that structure explicit."[11]

The Missing Processes in Learning

Reid Lyon criticizes whole language for what he says is its tenet that reading is "a natural process" similar to learning to speak and that children learn "naturally" in a literate environment. Aside from questions about the accuracy of this characterization, it is ironic that the body of research we have reviewed has its own very strong assumptions about the "natural" psychological processes in learning to read. The argument skills-emphasis proponents present that phonological awareness is the chief causal agent in learning to read and that children need first to learn the alphabetic principle posits a natural imperative—a belief that these initial steps are part of a largely invariant psychological process in achieving literacy. This assumption about this supposedly necessary, natural psychological step in early reading has contributed to a research methodology that stresses a singular progression of needs and minimizes variations in learning.

Predicated on its own theory of a natural and systematic learning process, the NICHD and related research have completely ignored how individuals might vary in their learning. A number of these studies distinguish children by subcategories, such as the different kinds of phonemic skills they possess that might differentiate them, but beyond these, the research offers information primarily on input and output. What actually happens as children are engaged with written language is not explained by this research. In fact, no child is ever described in these studies, only programs, subjects, controls, categories, and data—and nowhere is there an account of what is occurring while the children are learning. Some questions that might have rendered these studies more effective are:

- What kinds of interactions occur between the children and teachers that could impair or promote learning?
- How do children's interests contribute to the learning process?
- How does creative writing contribute to learning the alphabetic principle?
- How does work in the basal readers used in the studies contribute to or impair literacy learning for individual children?

These are only a handful of considerations a skilled teacher would have to address as part of effective teaching but which are omitted from the methodology of inordinate uniformity. More, much more than an exercise on diversity, understanding, and addressing the many facets of literacy education in which children may engage differently from one another, addressing uniqueness is an essential part of ensuring that all children learn to read.

Limiting Definitions of Scientific Knowledge

In an editorial on "science in modern life," the editor of *The Sciences*, a journal of the New York Academy of Sciences, addressed the question "What is the most important invention in the past two thousand years?" The question had been posed to an Internet discussion group and generated many "clever, provocative responses: the stirrup, the contraceptive pill, space travel." The editor's choice—and he was not alone—went to "a process still being invented: the scientific method." As an example, he pointed to a study on menstruation, noting that the researcher used "a novel scientific approach" consisting of an anthropologist living with a West African traditional society and noting and keeping track of menstrual cycles and the part menstruation had in culture. The anthropologist observed, collected data, and proposed a new theory of the evolution, biology, and culture of menstruation.[12]

The methodology that evoked such praise would never be in accord with the confined definition of "scientific study" of the research we have reviewed. Nonetheless, both the anthropological research and the editor's remarks illustrate not only that this kind of observational study is considered part of the "scientific method," but that the first step in scientific pursuits is to ask important questions. Only then can a researcher identify the best way to obtain evidence in a rigorous, organized, documentable way for addressing the questions.

Two Nobel Prize–winning physicists have been critical of the narrow definition of the scientific method such as that guiding all the studies we have reviewed. One declared that what has been called the scientific method can be used "for only quite simple problems." The other physicist, also criticizing the narrow conception of the scientific method, observed, "There is no scientific method as such, but the vital features of the scientist's procedure has been merely to do his utmost with his mind, *no holds barred.*"[13] We could add more, but the following is essential: scientific pursuits, especially in the human sciences, should not begin with the question "What important questions can we study that can be fit into the method we deem most rigorously scientific?"

Diminishing the Meaning of Literacy

Perhaps reasonably, the research we have reviewed assumes that the outcomes it identifies, such as reading real and nonsense words, reading and comprehending paragraphs, and so forth, are basic outcomes that can serve as measures for appraising the effectiveness of training programs and classroom reading instruction regardless of the form of instruction. After all, all instructional approaches have basic literacy outcomes in common. It might even seem reasonable to conclude, as the skills-emphasis researchers do, that other outcome goals can be added but remain nonetheless secondary to the fundamental goals of reading words, comprehending paragraphs, and so forth. If children cannot do the basic literacy tasks used in this research, after all, they will not be able to achieve these secondary goals either.

The problem with this explanation is precisely in its assumptions about satisfactory primary and secondary literacy goals: that is, it does not recognize that the "basic" outcome criteria of the research will inevitably encourage only those forms of instruction most closely directed toward achieving these outcome measures. Furthermore, the narrower the goals, the more they reinforce narrow instruction aimed at a narrow conception of children's education. However, once we establish other goals, derived from wider values, the outcome goals change accordingly because these seemingly separable goals are, from one educational view, inseparable.

Alternative Views and Policy

The NICHD and related research would also be of less concern if policy makers and legislators presented with it also had the opportunity to consider critical appraisals of it. Instead, although many investigators who have conducted these studies have insisted on "peer-review" as a sine qua non for published research—that is, having researchers familiar with an area of study evaluate the quality of a study and recommend whether or not it should be published—peer review has often been lacking in various decision-making processes in which NICHD and related reading research has been offered as evidence.[14]

I will end the book with a story that illustrates the contradiction between claims about this research being solely "science" and the disturbing actuality of a seamless connection between research, policy, and politics. It is a story about the Foorman study, to which I return one more time because of its extraordinary influence.

For more than a year before the Foorman study was actually published, it was used in media, policy, legislation, and a national report on reading. Explaining their decision not to make a manuscript of the study available to anyone who requested it, the authors said that guidelines of the American Psychological Association[15] (APA)—the organization that published the journal in which the manuscript was submitted—did not allow it. As Jack Fletcher, a coauthor of the paper, explained in an Internet discussion of the National Reading Conference a year prior to publication of the Foorman study, "The reason that we have not released the paper prior to publication was not to withhold data or information, but to prevent inappropriate use of the findings in this study and to observe APA guidelines."[16] In an e-mail to me, Barbara Foorman reiterated the explanation about not releasing the paper because of APA guidelines that are found, she said, "on the copyright page that APA has authors sign."[17]

A reading of the APA Publication Rights Form, however, reveals that the guidelines for distributing a prepublication paper are opposite of those described by Foorman and her colleagues. The agreement authors have to sign ("Section II—Copyright Transfer"), transferring the copyright to the APA, states that in return, the organization "grants the authors . . . permission to make limited distribution of all or portions of the above paper prior to publication." In other words, rather than preventing the authors from distributing the prepublication manuscript, the agreement actually gives them permission to do so, albeit limitedly. Anyone who has ever requested prepublication manuscripts, as I have, knows that limited distribution of professional papers is the norm. With respect to the researchers' fear that someone would make "inappropriate use of the findings," certainly, presenting the purported findings of the paper in the media and presenting them to policy makers, as Foorman and her colleagues did, without disseminating them to those who could criticize them, seems egregiously "inappropriate."

Conclusion

The subtitle of this book is *The Bad Science That Hurts Children*. In criticizing the research I have reviewed I am not proposing an anti-science position. Rather, the deficiencies in this research should actually suggest how good scientific study of reading might be achieved. I propose that scientific inquiries about learning to read begin with the end of this book's subtitle: a consideration of children and children's learning. What quality of life do we want for them? What life "burdens" do we not want them to shoulder? Toward what literacy education goals would we like them to strive? What personal qualities do we want to promote? What kind of critical thinkers do we want them to be? What kind of passions would we like them to have? What emotions do we want to encourage or discourage? Only as we work out these goals can we employ rigorous, systematic, creative, and varied scientific means to reach them.

Notes

Introduction

1. Goodman, K. S., P. Shannon, Y. S. Freeman, and S. Murphy. 1988. *Report Card on Basal Readers.* Katonah, NY: Richard C. Owen. (Quotation on p. 1.)

2. Moats, L. C. 1995. "The Missing Foundation in Teacher Education." *American Educator* 19 (Summer): 9–51. (Quotation on p. 9.)

3. Hall, S. L., and L. C. Moats. 1999. *Straight Talk About Reading: How Parents Can Make a Difference During the Early Years.* Chicago: Contemporary Books. (Quotation on p. 82.)

4. Adams, M. J., and M. Bruck. 1995. "Resolving the Great Debate." *American Educator* 19: 7–20. (Quotation on p. 15.)

5. Hall and Moats. *Straight Talk.* (Quotation on p. 112.)

6. Routman, R. 1996. *Literacy at the Crossroads: Critical Talk About Reading, Writing, and Other Teaching Dilemmas.* Portsmouth, NH: Heinemann. (Quotation on p. 42.)

7. Routman. *Literacy at the Crossroads.*

8. Church, S. M. 1996. *The Future of Whole Language: Reconstruction or Self-Destruction?* Portsmouth, NH: Heinemann. (Quotations on pp. 2–3.)

9. Coles, G. 1998. *Reading Lessons: The Debate over Literacy.* New York: Hill & Wang; McQuillan, J. 1998. *The Literacy Crisis: False Claims, Real Solutions.* Portsmouth, NH: Heinemann.

10. Paterson, F. R. R. 1998. "The Christian Right and the Prophonics Movement." ERIC NO: ED421779. Paper presented at the annual meeting of the American Educational Research Association.

11. Ohanian, S. 1999. *One Size Fits Few: The Folly of Educational Standards.* Portsmouth, NH: Heinemann, 96–100.

12. Sahagun, L. 1998. "L.A. Schools Chief Orders Phonics Lessons." *Los Angeles Times,* 7 November.

13. Helfand, D. 1999. "Reading Wars Rage on at Teachers Convention." *Los Angeles Times,* 5 May.

14. Wilgoren, D. 1998. "Raising Standards from Word One." *Washington Post,* 12 May.

15. Bowler, M. 1998. "Experts' Bias Complicates Lesson Debate." *Baltimore Sun*, 9 August.

16. Athans, M. 1998. "Texas Reading Scores Rocket." *Baltimore Sun*, 15 March.

17. Colvin, R. L., and R. T. Cooper. 1998. "Reading Moves to Front of the Class." *Los Angeles Times*, 27 September.

18. Ravitch, D. 1997. "Success in Brooklyn, But Not in D.C." *Forbes* (2 June): 112.

19. Goodman, K. 1998. "Comments on the Reading Excellence Act." *Reading Online* (<www.readingonline.org>).

20. Sweet, R. W. Jr. 1998. "The Reading Excellence Act: A Breakthrough for Reading Teacher Training." *Right to Read Report* 4: 1–5. (Quotation on p. 1.)

21. Mills, K. 1998. "Duane Alexander: Catching Kids Who Can't Read, a Guardian Extends His Reach." *Los Angeles Times*, 11 October.

22. Lyon, G. R. 1998. "Why Reading Is Not a Natural Process." *Educational Leadership* (March): 14–18. (Quotations on pp. 15, 18.)

23. Chase, A. 1975. *The Legacy of Malthus: The Social Costs of the New Scientific Racism*. New York: Knopf; Gould, S. J. 1981. *The Mismeasure of Man*. New York: W. W. Norton.

24. Sokal, A., and J. Bricmont. 1998. *Fashionable Nonsense: Postmodernism Intellectuals' Abuse of Science*. New York: Picador USA.

25. Krashen, S. D. 1999. *Three Arguments Against Whole Language and Why They Are Wrong*. Portsmouth, NH: Heinemann; Paulson, E. J., and K. S. Goodman. 1998. "Influential Studies in Eye-Movement Research." *Reading Online* (<www.readingonline.org/research/eyemove.html>); McQuillan. *The Literacy Crisis*.

26. Coles. *Reading Lessons*.

27. Goodman, K. S., ed. 1998. *In Defense of Good Teaching*. York, Maine: Stenhouse Publishers; Taylor, D. 1998. *Beginning to Read and the Spin Doctors of Science*. Urbana, IL: National Council of Teachers of English.

28. Schwebel, M. 1968. *Who Can Be Educated?* New York: Grove Press.

29. Schwebel. *Who Can Be Educated?* (Quotation on p. 37.)

Chapter 1

1. Coles, G. 1987. *The Learning Mystique: A Critical Look at "Learning Disabilities."* New York: Pantheon; Coles, G. 1998. *Reading Lessons: The Debate Over Literacy*. New York: Hill & Wang.

2. Flesch, R. 1955. *Why Johnny Can't Read*. New York: Harper & Row. (Quotation on p. 2.)

3. Flesch, R. 1981. *Why Johnny Still Can't Read: A New Look at the Scandal of Our Schools*. New York: Harper & Row.

4. Chall, J. 1967. *Learning to Read: The Great Debate.* New York: McGraw-Hill. (Quotations on p. 75.)

5. Anderson, R. C., E. H. Hiebert, J. A. Scott, and I. A. Wilkinson. 1985. *Becoming a Nation of Readers: The Report of the Commission on Reading.* Washington, D.C.: National Institute of Education. (Quotation on p. 37.)

6. Bennett, W. J. 1986. *First Lessons: A Report on Elementary Education in America.* Washington, D.C.: U.S. Department of Education; Bennett, W. J. 1986. *What Works: Research About Teaching and Learning.* Washington, D.C.: U.S. Department of Education.

7. Lyon, G. R. 1996. "Learning Disabilities." *The Future of Children* 6 (Spring): 54–76. (Quotations on pp. 64–65.)

8. Shaywitz, B. A., S. E. Shaywitz, J. M. Fletcher, K. R. Pugh, J. C. Gore, et al. 1997. "The Yale Center for the Study of Learning and Attention: Longitudinal and Neurobiological Studies." *Learning Disabilities* 8 (Winter): 21–29. (Quotation on p. 23.)

9. Stanovich, K. E. 1993/1994. "Romance and Reality." *Reading Teacher* 47 (December/January): 280–91. (Quotation on p. 283.)

10. Stanovich, K. E., A. E. Cunningham, and B. B. Cramer. 1984. "Assessing Phonological Awareness in Kindergarten Children: Issues of Task Comparability." *Journal of Experimental Child Psychology* 38: 175–90.

11. Stanovich, Cunningham, and Cramer. "Assessing Phonological Awareness." (Quotations on pp. 188–89.)

12. Stanovich, Cunningham, and Cramer. "Assessing Phonological Awareness." (Quotation on p. 189.)

13. Treiman, R., and J. Baron. 1983. "Phonemic-Analysis Training Helps Children Benefit from Spelling-Sound Rules." *Memory and Cognition* 11: 382–89. (Quotation on p. 384.)

14. Treiman and Baron. "Phonemic-Analysis Training." (Quotation on p. 388.)

15. Stanovich, Cunningham, and Cramer. "Assessing Phonological Awareness." (Quotation on p. 189.)

16. Bradley, L., and P. Bryant. 1983. "Categorizing Sounds and Learning to Read: A Causal Connection." *Nature* 301: 419–21.

17. Stanovich, K. E., A. E. Cunningham, and D. J. Feeman. 1984. "Intelligence, Cognitive Skills, and Early Reading Progress." *Reading Research Quarterly* 19: 278–303.

18. Stanovich, Cunningham, and Feeman. "Intelligence." (Quotation on p. 297.)

19. Fox, B., and D. K. Routh. 1980. "Phonemic Analysis and Severe Reading Disability in Children." *Journal of Psycholinguistic Research* 9: 115–19. (Quotations on pp. 118–19.)

20. Fox, B., and D. K. Routh. 1983. "Reading Disability, Phonemic Analysis, and Dysphonetic Spelling: A Follow-Up Study." *Journal of Clinical Child Psychology* 12: 28–32. (Quotation on p. 31.)

21. Perfetti, C. A., I. Beck, L. C. Bell, and C. Hughes. 1987. "Phonemic Knowledge and Learning to Read Are Reciprocal: A Longitudinal Study of First Grade Children." *Merrill-Palmer Quarterly* 33: 283–319. (Quotation on p. 309.)

22. Perfetti et al. "Phonemic Knowledge." (Quotation on. p. 290.)

23. Perfetti et al. "Phonemic Knowledge." (Quotations on p. 317.)

24. Perfetti et al. "Phonemic Knowledge." (Quotation on p. 315.)

25. Stanovich, K. E. 1993. "A Model for Studies of Reading Disability." *Developmental Review* 13: 225–45. (Quotation on p. 227.)

26. Calfee, R. C., P. Lindamood, and C. Lindamood. 1973. "Acoustic-Phonetic Skills and Reading—Kindergarten Through Twelfth Grade." *Journal of Educational Psychology* 64: 293–98.

27. Stanovich, Cunningham, and Feeman. "Intelligence." (Quotation on p. 283.)

28. Calfee, Lindamood, and Lindamood. "Acoustic-Phonetic Skills." (Quotation on p. 298.)

29. Stanovich, K. E. 1986. "Matthew Effects in Reading: Some Consequences of Individual Differences in the Acquisition of Literacy." *Reading Research Quarterly* 21: 360–406.

30. Stanovich. "Matthew Effects." (Quotations on p. 362.)

31. Stanovich, Cunningham, and Cramer. "Assessing Phonological Awareness"; Stanovich, Cunningham, and Feeman. "Intelligence."

32. Share, D. L., A. F. Jorm, R. Maclean, and R. Matthews. 1984. "Sources of Individual Differences in Reading Acquisition." *Journal of Educational Psychology* 76: 1309–24. (Quotation on p. 1313.)

33. Share et al. "Sources of Individual Differences." (Quotation on p. 1322.)

34. Share et al. "Sources of Individual Differences." (Quotation on p. 1313.)

35. Stanovich. "Matthew Effects." (Quotations on p. 363.)

36. Stanovich. "Matthew Effects." (Quotations on p. 363.)

37. Torneus, M. 1984. "Phonological Awareness and Reading: A Chicken and Egg Problem?" *Journal of Educational Psychology* 6: 1346–58. (Quotation on p. 1355.)

38. Torneus. "Phonological Awareness." (Quotation on p. 1355.)

39. Olofsson, A., and I. Lundberg. 1983. "Can Phonemic Awareness Be Trained in Kindergarten?" *Scandinavian Journal of Psychology* 24: 35–44; Olofsson, A., and I. Lundberg. 1985. "Evaluation of Long Term Effects of Phonemic Awareness Training in Kindergarten: Illustrations of Some Methodological Problems in Evaluation Research." *Scandinavian Journal of Psychology* 26: 21–34.

40. Olofsson and Lundberg. "Can Phonemic Awareness Be Trained?" (Quotation on p. 37.)

41. Olofsson and Lundberg. "Long Term Effects." (Quotation on p. 31.)

42. Stanovich. "Matthew Effects." (Quotation on p. 363.)

43. Stanovich. "Romance and Reality." (Quotation on p. 287.)

44. Adams, M. J., B. R. Foorman, I. Lundberg, and T. Beeler. 1998. "The Elusive Phoneme." *American Educator* (Spring/Summer): 18–29. (Quotation on p. 20.)

Chapter 2

1. Fletcher, J. M., and G. R. Lyon. 1998. "Reading: A Research-Based Approach." In *What's Gone Wrong in America's Classrooms*, ed. W. M. Evers, 49–90. Stanford, CA: Hoover Institution Press. (Quotation on p. 50.)

2. Lyon, G. R. 1997. Testimony of G. Reid Lyon on Children's Literacy. Committee on Education and the Workforce, U.S. House of Representatives, Washington, D.C.

3. Lyon. Testimony.

4. Lyon. Testimony.

5. Lyon, G. R. 1998. "Why Reading Is Not a Natural Process." *Educational Leadership* March: 14–18. (Quotation on p. 18.)

6. Fletcher and Lyon. "Reading." (Quotation on pp. 77–78.)

7. Lyon, G. R., and L. C. Moats. 1997. "Critical Conceptual and Methodological Considerations in Reading Intervention Research." *Journal of Learning Disabilities* 30: 578–88. (Quotation on p. 578.)

8. Foorman, B. R., D. J. Francis, D. Winikates, P. Mehta, C. Schatschneider, and J. M. Fletcher. 1997. "Early Interventions for Children with Reading Disabilities." *Scientific Studies of Reading* 3: 255–76.

9. Foorman et al. "Early Interventions." (Quotation on p. 260.)

10. Foorman et al. "Early Interventions." (Quotations on pp. 258, 272.)

11. Foorman et al. "Early Interventions." (Quotation on p. 272.)

12. Lyon and Moats. "Conceptual and Methodological Considerations." (Quotation on p. 578.)

13. Lyon and Moats. "Conceptual and Methodological Considerations." (Quotation on p. 578.)

14. Torgesen, J. K., R. K. Wagner, C. A. Rashotte, A. W. Alexander, and T. Conway. 1997. "Preventative and Remedial Interventions for Children with Severe Reading Disabilities." *Learning Disabilities: A Multidisciplinary Journal* 8: 51–62. (Quotations on p. 54.)

15. Torgesen et al. "Preventative and Remedial Interventions." (Quotation on p. 55.)

16. Fletcher and Lyon. "Reading." (Quotation on p. 67.)

17. Torgesen, J. K., R. K. Wagner, and C. A. Rashotte. 1997. "Prevention and

Remediation of Severe Reading Disabilities: Keeping the End in Mind." *Scientific Studies in Reading* 1: 217–34. (Quotation on p. 225.)

18. Torgesen, J. K., R. K. Wagner, C. A. Rashotte. "Preventing Reading Failure in Young Children with Phonological Processing Disabilities: Group and Individual Responses to Instruction." *Journal of Educational Psychology* (in press).

19. Torgesen et al. "Preventative and Remedial Interventions." (Quotations on p. 57.)

20. Lovett, M. W., S. L. Borden, T. DeLuca, L. Lacerenza, N. J. Benson, and D. Brackstone. 1994. "Treating the Core Deficits of Developmental Dyslexia: Evidence of Transfer of Learning After Phonologically- and Strategy-Based Reading Training Programs." *Developmental Psychology* 30: 805–22.

21. Torgesen, Wagner, and Rashotte. "Prevention and Remediation." (Quotation on p. 220.)

22. Lyon and Moats. "Conceptual and Methodological Considerations." (Quotations on p. 578.)

23. Olson, R. K., B. Wise, J. Ring, and M. Johnson. 1997. "Computer-Based Remedial Training in Phoneme Awareness and Phonological Decoding: Effects on the Posttraining Development of Word Recognition." *Scientific Studies of Reading* 1: 235–53. (Quotation on p. 239.)

24. Wise, B. W., and R. Olson. 1995. "Computer-Based Phonological Awareness and Reading Instruction." *Annals of Dyslexia* 45: 99–122. (Quotation on p. 117.)

25. Olson et al. "Computer-Based Training." (Quotations on pp. 236, 246, my emphasis.)

26. Olson et al. "Computer-Based Training." (Quotations on pp. 249–50.)

27. Castles, A., and M. Coltheart. 1993. "Varieties of Developmental Dyslexia." *Cognition* 47: 149–80.

28. Vellutino, F. R., D. M. Scanlon, E. R. Sipay, S. G. Small, A. Pratt, R. Chen, and M. B. Denckla. 1996. "Cognitive Profiles of Difficult-to-Remediate and Readily Remediated Poor Readers: Early Intervention as a Vehicle for Distinguishing Between Cognitive and Experiential Deficits as Basic Causes of Specific Reading Disability." *Journal of Educational Psychology* 88 (4): 601–38. (Quotations on p. 610.)

29. Fletcher and Lyon. "Reading." (Quotation on p. 68.)

30. Fletcher and Lyon. "Reading." (Quotation on p. 68.)

31. Vellutino et al. "Cognitive Profiles." (Quotations on pp. 610, 612.)

32. Vellutino et al. "Cognitive Profiles." (Quotation on p. 630.)

33. Scanlon, D. M., and F. R. Vellutino. 1997. "A Comparison of the Instructional Backgrounds and Cognitive Profiles of Poor, Average, and Good Readers Who Were Initially Identified as at Risk for Reading Failure." *Scientific Studies in Reading* 3: 191–215. (Quotation on p. 193.)

34. Brady, S., A. Fowler, B. Stone, and N. Winbury. 1994. "Training Phonological Awareness: A Study with Inner-City Kindergarten Children." *Annals of Dyslexia* 44: 26–59. (Quotation on p. 30.)

35. Brady et al. "Training Phonological Awareness." (Quotations on pp. 44–45.)

36. Brady et al. "Training Phonological Awareness." (Quotations on pp. 46–47.)

37. Brady et al. "Training Phonological Awareness." (Quotation on p. 48.)

38. Fletcher and Lyon. "Reading." (Quotations on pp. 64–65.)

39. Felton, R. H. 1993. "Effects of Instruction on the Decoding Skills of Children with Phonological Processing Problems." *Journal of Learning Disabilities* 26: 583–89. (Quotations on pp. 584, 585.); Brown, I. S., and R. H. Felton. 1990. "Effects of Instruction on Beginning Reading Skills in Children at Risk for Reading Disability." *Reading and Writing* 2: 223–41.

40. Houghton Mifflin Co. 1986. *Houghton Mifflin Reading.* Boston: Houghton Mifflin Co.

41. Macmillan Publishing Co. 1981. *Lippincott Basic Reading.* Riverside, NJ: Macmillan Publishing Co.

42. Felton. "Effects." (Quotations on p. 585.)

43. Felton. "Effects." (Quotation on p. 585.)

44. Fletcher and Lyon. "Reading." (Quotation on p. 65.)

45. Goodman, K. S., P. Shannon, Y. S. Freeman, and S. Murphy. 1988. *Report Card on Basal Readers.* Katonah, NY: Richard C. Owen. (Quotations on pp. 71–72, 100.)

46. Lyon and Moats. "Conceptual and Methodological Considerations." (Quotation on p. 579.)

47. Fletcher and Lyon. "Reading." (Quotations on p. 51.)

48. Lyon. Testimony.

49. Lyon, G. R., and C. Vinita. 1996. "The Current State of Science and the Future of Specific Reading Disability." *Mental Retardation and Developmental Disabilities Research Reviews* 2: 2–9. (Quotation on p. 4.)

Chapter 3

1. Anderluh, D. 1998. "Building with Words: City Schools Hope Phonics Boosts Reading." *Sacramento Bee*, 1 February.

2. Anderluh. "Building with Words."

3. Foorman, B. R., D. J. Francis, J. M. Fletcher, and C. Schatschneider. 1998. "The Role of Instruction in Learning to Read: Preventing Reading Failure in At-Risk Children." *Journal of Educational Psychology* 90: 37–55.

4. Foorman et al. "The Role of Instruction." (Quotations on p. 39.)

5. Foorman et al. "The Role of Instruction." (Quotation on p. 40.)

6. Foorman et al. "The Role of Instruction." (Quotations on pp. 40, 51.)

7. Kaufman, A. S., and N. L. Kaufman. 1985. *Kaufman Test of Educational Achievement.* Circle Pines, MN: American Guidance Service.

8. Woodcock, R. W., and M. B. Johnson. 1989. *Woodcock-Johnson Psychoeducational Battery—Revised.* Allen, TX: DLM Teaching Resources.

9. Foorman et al. "The Role of Instruction." (Quotations on pp. 50, 51.)

10. Foorman et al. "The Role of Instruction." (Quotations on pp. 50, 51.)

11. Wiederholt, J. L. 1986. *Formal Reading Inventory: A Method for Assessing Silent Reading Comprehension and Oral Reading Miscues.* Austin, TX: Pro-Ed.

12. Foorman et al. "The Role of Instruction." (Quotation on p. 52.)

13. Foorman, B. R., D. J. Francis, T. Beeler, D. Winikates, and J. Fletcher. 1997. "Early Interventions for Children with Reading Problems: Study Designs and Preliminary Findings." *Learning Disabilities* 8 (Winter): 63–71. (Quotation on p. 68.)

14. Wiederholt. *Formal Reading Inventory.* (Quotation on p. 13.)

15. Wiederholt. *Formal Reading Inventory.* (Quotation on p. 16.)

16. Fletcher, J. 1998. Internet post on the National Reading Conference listserv, 10 April.

17. Foorman et al. "The Role of Instruction." (Quotation on p. 40.)

18. Snow, C. E., M. S. Burns, and P. Griffin, eds. 1998. *Preventing Reading Difficulties in Young Children.* Washington, D.C.: National Academy Press.

19. Snow, Burns, and Griffin. *Preventing Reading Difficulties.* (Quotation on p. 206.)

20. Strauss, S. 1997. "Phonics Reading Method Best, Study Finds: Whole Language Approach Significantly Less Effective, Houston Research Shows." *The Toronto Globe and Mail,* 18 February.

Chapter 4

1. Adams, M. 1997. Internet post on the Teachers Applying Whole Language listserv, 1 April.

2. Adams, M. 1997. Internet post on the Teachers Applying Whole Language listserv, 9 April.

3. Foorman, B. 1998. Personal communication, 10 October.

4. Adams, M. J., B. R. Foorman, I. Lundberg, and T. Beeler. 1998. *Phonemic Awareness in Young Children: A Classroom Curriculum.* Baltimore: Paul H. Brookes.

5. Adams, M. 1997. Internet post on the Teachers Applying Whole Language listserv, 20 April 20.

6. McPike, E. 1998. Introduction to Adams, M. J., B. R. Foorman, I. Lundberg, and T. Beeler. "The Elusive Phoneme." *American Educator* 22 (Spring/Summer): 18–19. (Quotation on p. 19.)

7. Foorman, B. R., L. Jenkins, and D. J. Francis. 1993. "Links Among Segmenting, Spelling, and Reading Words in First and Second Grades." *Reading and Writing* 5: 1–15. (Quotation on p. 1.)

8. Adams, M. J., B. R. Foorman, I. Lundberg, and T. Beeler. "The Elusive Phoneme." *American Educator* 22 (Spring/Summer): 18–29. (Quotation on p. 19.)

9. Lundberg, I., J. Frost, and O-P. Petersen. 1988. "Effects of an Extensive Program for Stimulating Phonological Awareness in Preschool Children." *Reading Research Quarterly* 23: 263–84.

10. Olofsson, A., and I. Lundberg. 1983. "Can Phonemic Awareness Be Trained in Kindergarten?" *Scandinavian Journal of Psychology* 24: 35–44; Olofsson, A., and I. Lundberg. 1985. "Evaluation of Long Term Effects of Phonemic Awareness Training in Kindergarten: Illustrations of Some Methodological Problems in Evaluation Research." *Scandinavian Journal of Psychology* 26: 21–34.

11. Lundberg, Frost, and Petersen. "Effects of an Extensive Program." (Quotations on pp. 267–68.)

12. Adams et al. "The Elusive Phoneme." (Quotation on p. 20.)

13. Lundberg, I., A. Olofsson, and S. Wall. 1980. "Reading and Spelling Skills in the First School Years Predicted from Phonemic Awareness Skills in Kindergarten." *Scandinavian Journal of Psychology* 21: 159–73.

14. Wagner, R. K., and J. K. Torgesen. 1987. "The Nature of Phonological Processing and Its Causal Role in the Acquisition of Reading Skills." *Psychological Bulletin* 101: 192–212. (Quotation on p. 199.)

15. Hoien, T., I. Lundberg, K. E. Stanovich, and I. Bjaalid. 1995. "Components of Phonological Awareness." *Reading and Writing* 7: 171–88.

16. Adams et al. "The Elusive Phoneme." (Quotation on p. 20.)

17. Foorman, B. R., D. J. Francis, T. Beeler, D. Winikates, and J. Fletcher. "Early Interventions for Children with Reading Problems: Study Designs and Preliminary Findings." *Learning Disabilities* 8: 63–71.

18. Lyon, G. R., and L. C. Moats. 1997. "Critical Conceptual and Methodological Considerations in Reading Intervention Research." *Journal of Learning Disabilities* 30: 578–88. (Quotation on p. 578.)

19. Foorman et al. "Early Interventions." (Quotations on p. 65.)

20. Foorman, B. R., D. J. Francis, S. E. Shaywitz, B. A. Shaywitz, and J. M. Fletcher. 1997. "The Case for Early Reading Intervention." In *Foundations of Reading Acquisition and Dyslexia: Implications for Early Intervention*, ed. B. Blachman, 243–64. Mahwah, NJ: Lawrence Erlbaum Associates.

21. Foorman, B. 1998. Personal communication. 20 October.

22. Byrne, B., and R. Fielding-Barnsley. 1991. "Evaluation of a Program to Teach Phonemic Awareness to Young Children." *Journal of Educational Psychology* 83: 451–55; Byrne, B., and R. Fielding-Barnsley. 1993. "Evaluation of a Program to Teach Phonemic Awareness to Young Children: A 1-Year Follow-Up." *Journal of Educational Psychology* 85: 104–11; Byrne, B., and R. Fielding-Barnsley. 1995. "Evaluation of a Program to Teach Phonemic Awareness to Young Children: A 2- and 3-Year Follow-Up and a New Preschool Trial." *Journal of Educational Psychology* 88: 18–37.

23. Adams et al. "The Elusive Phoneme."

24. Coles, G. 1987. *The Learning Mystique: A Critical Look at "Learning Disabilities."* New York: Pantheon, 76–77.

25. Adams et al. "The Elusive Phoneme." (Quotation on p. 19.)

26. Wagner, R. K., J. K. Torgesen, and C. A. Rashotte. 1994. "Development of Reading-Related Phonological Abilities: New Evidence of Bidirectional Causality from a Latent Variable Longitudinal Study." *Developmental Psychology* 30: 73–87. (Quotation on p. 84.)

27. Ball, E. W., and B. A. Blachman. 1991. "Does Phoneme Awareness Training in Kindergarten Make a Difference in Early Word Recognition and Developmental Spelling?" *Reading Research Quarterly* 26: 49–66. (Quotation on p. 63.)

28. Blachman, B., E. Ball, R. Black, and D. Tangel. 1994. "Kindergarten Teachers Develop Phoneme Awareness in Low-Income, Inner-City Classrooms." *Reading and Writing* 6: 1–18.

29. Adams et al. "The Elusive Phoneme." (Quotation on p. 20.)

30. Castle, J. M., J. Riach, and T. Nicholson. 1994. "Getting Off to a Better Start in Reading and Spelling: The Effect of Phonemic Awareness Instruction Within a Whole Language Program." *Journal of Experimental Psychology* 86: 350–59. (Quotations on pp. 350–51.)

Chapter 5

1. Bowler, M. 1999. "Phonics Experiment Has Sound of Success." *Baltimore Sun*, 7 February.

2. Bowler, M. 1999. Personal communication. 13 February.

3. Internet address: <www.sra-4kids/index2.html>. Click on *reading* then on *Open Court*.

4. SRA/McGraw-Hill. 1999. *Research Related to Open Court Collections for Young Scholars*. Mahway, NJ: SRA/McGraw-Hill.

5. Siegel, J. 1997. "The Jewel in the Crown." *Teacher Magazine* 9 (October): 24–29. (Quotations on p. 25.)

6. Adams, M. 1997. Internet post on the Teachers Applying Whole Language listserv, 8 April. (Emphasis in original.)

7. Ravitch, D. 1997. "Success in Brooklyn, but Not in D.C." *Forbes* (2 June): 112. (Quotations on p. 112.)

8. The miscellaneous materials contained in the publisher's packet do not have special labels and have no page numbers.

9. McQuillan, J. 1998. Internet post on California Association of Teachers of English listserv (CATEnet), 15 September.

Chapter 6

1. Manzo, K. K. 1998. "Study Finds Distinctive Brain Patterns in People with Dyslexia." *Education Week*, 11 March.

2. Kolata, G. 1998. "Scientists Track the Process of Reading Through the Brain." *New York Times*, 3 March.

3. Shaywitz, S., and G. R. Lyon. 1998. "Unscrambling Dyslexia." Interview by J. Lehrer. *The NewsHour with Jim Lehrer*. Public Broadcasting System, 11 March.

4. For example: Recer, P. 1998. "Study: Dyslexia Is Biological." Associated Press, 3 March; "Brain 'Signature' for Dyslexia Found." 1998. *UPI Science News*, 2 March; Suplee, C. "Clue to Dyslexia Found." *Washington Post*, 3 March; "Distinctive Brain Pattern Found for Dyslexia." 1998. Reuters, 3 March; "Biological Basis for Reading Disabilities Discovered." 1998. *PRNewswire*, 2 March.

5. Lyon, G. R. 1995. "Research Initiatives in Learning Disabilities: Contributions from Scientists Supported by the National Institute of Child Health and Human Development." *Journal of Child Neurology* 10 (January): S120–26. (Quotation on p. S124.)

6. Lyon, G. R., D. Alexander, and S. Yaffe. 1997. "Progress and Promise in Research in Learning Disabilities." *Learning Disabilities* 8 (1): 1–6. (Quotation on p. 4.)

7. Lyon, G. R. 1996. "Learning Disabilities." *The Future of Children* 6 (Spring): 54–76. (Quotation on p. 65.)

8. Lyon, G. R. 1996. "Why Johnny Can't Decode." *Washington Post*, 27 October.

9. Coles, G. 1998. *Reading Lessons: The Debate over Literacy*. New York: Hill & Wang, Ch. 7.

10. Shaywitz, S. E., B. A. Shaywitz, K. R. Pugh, R. K. Fulbright, R. T. Constable, W. E. Mencl, D. P. Shankweiler, A. M. Liberman, P. Skudlarski, J. M. Fletcher, L. Katz, K. E. Marchione, C. Lacadie, C. Gatenby, and J. C. Gore. 1998. "Functional Disruption in the Organization of the Brain for Reading in Dyslexia." *Proceedings of the National Academy of Sciences* 95: 2636–41. (Quotation on p. 2636.)

11. Shaywitz and Lyon. "Unscrambling Dyslexia."

12. Shaywitz and Lyon. "Unscrambling Dyslexia."

13. Shaywitz and Lyon. "Unscrambling Dyslexia."

14. For example: Ruddell, R. B., M. R. Ruddell, and H. Singer, eds. 1994. *Theoretical Models and Processes of Reading, Fourth Edition*. Newark, DE: International Reading Association.

15. Shaywitz et al. "Functional Disruption." (Quotation on p. 2637.)

16. Shaywitz et al. "Functional Disruption." (Quotations on p. 2640.)

17. Shaywitz et al. "Functional Disruption." (Quotations on pp. 2638–40.)

18. Coles, G. S. 1987. *The Learning Mystique: A Critical Look at "Learning Disabilities."* New York: Pantheon.

19. Coles. *Reading Lessons*. Ch. 4.

20. Coles, G. S., and L. Goldstein. 1985. "Hemispheric EEG Activation and Literacy Development." *International Journal of Clinical Neuropsychology* 7: 3–7.

21. Hotz, R. L. 1998. "In Art of Language, the Brain Matters." *Los Angeles Times*, 18 October.

Chapter 7

1. "Genetic Root Found for Reading Disorder." 1994. Associated Press, 14 October.

2. "Researchers Pinpoint Gene for Dyslexia." 1994. Reuters, 14 October.

3. Blakeslee, S. 1994. "Researchers Find Gene That May Link Dyslexia with Immune Disorders." *New York Times*, 18 October.

4. Schnaiberg, L. 1994. "Study Adds to Evidence of Genetic Link to Dyslexia." *Education Week*, 26 October.

5. Lyon, G. R., D. Alexander, and S. Yaffe. 1997. "Progress and Promise in Research in Learning Disabilities." *Learning Disabilities* 8 (1): 1–6. (Quotation on p. 4.)

6. Lyon, G. R. 1996. "Learning Disabilities." *The Future of Children* 6 (Spring): 54–76. (Quotation on p. 65.)

7. Lyon, G. R. 1997. Testimony of G. Reid Lyon on Children's Literacy. Committee on Education and the Workforce, U.S. House of Representatives, Washington, D.C.

8. Coles, G. 1987. *The Learning Mystique: A Critical Look at "Learning Disabilities."* New York: Pantheon, Ch. 6.

9. Rack, John P., and R. K. Olson. 1993. "Phonological Deficits, IQ, and Individual Differences in Reading Disability: Genetic and Environmental Influences." *Developmental Review* 13: 269–73.

10. Cardon, L. R., S. D. Smith, D. W. Fulker, W. J. Kimberling, B. F. Pennington, and J. C. DeFries. 1994. "Quantitative Trait Locus for Reading Disability on CChromosome 6." *Science* 266 (14 October): 276–79.

11. Cardon et al. 1994. "Quantitative Trait Locus." (Quotations on p. 276.)

12. Cardon et al. 1994. "Quantitative Trait Locus." (Quotation on p. 278, Figure 2A.)

13. Cardon et al. 1994. "Quantitative Trait Locus." (Quotation on p. 279.)

14. Cardon, L. R., S. D. Smith, D. W. Fulker, W. J. Kimberling, B. F. Pennington, J. C. DeFries. 1995. "Quantitative Trait Locus for Reading Disability: Correction." *Science* 268 (16 June): 1553. (Quotation on p. 1553.)

15. Cardon et al. 1994. "Quantitative Trait Locus." (Quotation on p. 276.)

16. Cardon et al. 1995. "Quantitative Trait Locus: Correction." (Quotation on p. 1553.)

17. Coles. *The Learning Mystique*, Ch. 6.

18. DeFries, J. C., P. A. Filipek, D. W. Fulker, R. K. Olson, B. F. Pennington, S. D. Smith, and B. W. Wise. 1997. "Colorado Learning Disabilities Research Center." *Learning Disabilities* 8 (Winter): 7–19.

19. DeFries et al. "Colorado Learning Disabilities." (Quotation on p. 14.)

20. Grigorenko, E. L., F. B. Wood, M. S. Meyer, L. A. Hart, W. C. Speed, A. Shuster. 1997. "Susceptibility Loci for Chromosomes 6 and 15." *American Journal of Human Genetics* 60: 27–39. (Quotation on p. 30.)

21. Cardon et al. 1994. "Quantitative Trait Locus."

22. DeFries et al. "Colorado Learning Disabilities."

23. Cardon et al. 1994. "Quantitative Trait Locus." (Quotation on p. 278, Figure 4.)

24. Cardon et al. 1994. "Quantitative Trait Locus."

25. Grigorenko et al. "Susceptibility Loci." (Quotation on p. 29.)

26. Grigorenko et al. "Susceptibility Loci." (Quotation on p. 36.)

27. Grigorenko et al. "Susceptibility Loci." (Quotation on p. 34.)

28. Lieberman, P. 1998. *Eve Spoke: Human Language and Human Evolution.* New York: W. W. Norton. (Quotation on p. 129.)

29. Lieberman. *Eve Spoke.* (Quotations on p. 132.)

30. Coles, G. 1998. *Reading Lessons: The Debate over Literacy.* New York: Hill & Wang.

31. Lieberman. *Eve Spoke.* (Quotations on p. 132.)

Chapter 8

1. Cunningham, A. E. 1990. "Explicit Versus Implicit Instruction in Phonemic Awareness." *Journal of Experimental Child Psychology* 50: 429–44. (Quotations on p. 435.)

2. Brennan, F., and J. Ireson. 1997. "Training Phonological Awareness: A Study to Evaluate the Effects of a Program of Metalinguistic Games in Kindergarten." *Reading and Writing* 9: 241–63. (Quotation on p. 242.)

3. Brennan and Ireson. "Training Phonological Awareness." (Quotations on pp. 251, 257.)

4. Brennan and Ireson. "Training Phonological Awareness." (Quotations on p. 257.)

5. Hatcher, P. J., C. Hulme, and A. W. Ellis. 1994. "Ameliorating Early Reading Failure by Integrating the Teaching of Reading and Phonological Skills: The Phonological Linkage Hypothesis." *Child Development* 65: 41–57.

6. Hatcher, Hulme, and Ellis. "Ameliorating Early Reading Failure." (Quotations on pp. 52, 53.)

7. Lie, A. 1991. "Effects of a Training Program for Stimulating Skills in Word Analysis in First-Grade Children." *Reading Research Quarterly* 26: 234–50.

8. Schneider, W., P. Kuspet, E. Roth, and M. Vise. 1997. "Short- and Long-Term Effects of Training Phonological Awareness in Kindergarten: Evidence from Two German Studies." *Journal of Experimental Child Psychology* 66: 311–40. (Quotation on p. 321.)

9. Schneider et al. "Short- and Long-Term Effects." (Quotations on pp. 323–24.)

10. Schneider et al. "Short- and Long-Term Effects of Training Phonological Awareness." (Quotation on p. 333.)

11. Schneider et al. "Short- and Long-Term Effects of Training Phonological Awareness." (Quotations on p. 328.)

12. Hurford, D. P. 1990. "Training Phonemic Segmentation Ability with a Phonemic Discrimination Intervention in Second- and Third-Grade Children with Reading Disabilities." *Journal of Learning Disabilities* 23: 564–69.

13. Bryant, P., M. Maclean, and L. Bradley. 1990. "Rhyme, Language, and Children's Reading." *Applied Psycholinguistics* 11: 237–52. (Quotations on p. 245.)

14. Bryant, Maclean, and Bradley. "Rhyme." (Quotation on p. 239.)

15. Coles, G. 1998. *Reading Lessons: The Debate over Literacy.* New York: Hill & Wang, Ch. 3.

16. For example: O'Conner, R. E., J. R. Jenkins, and T. Slocum. 1995. "Transfer Among Phonological Tasks in Kindergarten: Essential Instructional Content." *Journal of Educational Psychology* 87: 202–17; Foster, K. C., G. C. Erickson, D. F. Foster, D. Brinkman, and J. K. Torgesen. 1994. "Computer Administered Instruction in Phonological Awareness: Evaluation of the Daisyquest Program." *Journal of Research and Development in Education* 27: 126–37; Slocum, T. A., R. E. O'Connor, and J. R. Jenkins. 1993. "Transfer Among Phonological Manipulation Skills." *Journal of Educational Psychology* 85: 618–30; Tangel, D. M., and B. A. Blachman. 1992. "Effect of Phoneme Awareness Instruction on Kindergarten Children's Invented Spelling." *Journal of Reading Behavior* 24: 233–61; Cary, L., and A. Verhaeghe. 1994. "Promoting Phonemic Analysis Ability Among Kindergartners." *Reading and Writing* 6: 251–78.

Chapter 9

1. Lyon, G. R. 1997. Testimony of G. Reid Lyon on Children's Literacy. Committee on Education and the Workforce, U.S. House of Representatives, Washington, D.C. (My emphasis.)

2. Adams, M. J., B. R. Foorman, I. Lundberg, and T. Beeler. 1998. "The Elusive Phoneme." *American Educator* 22 (Spring/Summer): 18–29. (Quotation on p. 19.)

3. Brady, S., A. Fowler, B. Stone, and N. Winbury. 1994. "Training Phonological Awareness: A Study with Inner-City Kindergarten Children." *Annals of Dyslexia* 44: 26–59. (Quotations on p. 30.)

4. Lyon, G. R. 1998. "Why Reading Is Not a Natural Process." *Educational Leadership* March: 14–18. (Quotations on p. 17.)

5. Wallach, L., M. A. Wallach, M. G. Dozier, and N. E. Kaplan. 1977. "Poor Children Learning to Read Do Not Have Trouble with Auditory Discrimination But Do Have Trouble with Phoneme Recognition." *Journal of Educational Psychology* 69: 36–39. (Quotations on pp. 37–38.)

6. Bowey, J. A. 1995. "Socioeconomic Status Differences in Preschool Phonological Sensitivity and First-Grade Reading Achievement." *Journal of Educational Psychology* 87: 476–87. (Quotation on p. 476.)

7. Lonigan, C. J., S. R. Burgess, J. L. Anthony, and T. A. Barker. 1998. "Development of Phonological Sensitivity in 2- to 5-Year-Old Children." *Journal of Educational Psychology* 90: 294–311.

8. Lonigan et al. "Development of Phonological Sensitivity." (Quotations on pp. 305–307.)

9. Adams, M. J. 1990. *Beginning to Read: Thinking and Learning About Print.* Cambridge, MA: MIT Press. (Quotations on p. 82.)

10. Adams. *Beginning to Read.* (Quotations on p. 84.)

11. For example: Wells, G. 1985. "Preschool Literacy-Related Activities and Success in School." In *Literacy, Language, and Learning,* ed. D. R. Olson, N. Torrance, and A. Hildyard, 229–55. New York: Cambridge University Press; Sulzby, E. 1985. "Children's Emergent Reading of Favorite Storybooks: A Developmental Study." *Reading Research Quarterly* 20: 458–81; Purcell-Gates, V. 1988. "Lexical and Syntactic Knowledge of Written Narrative Held by Well-Read-to Kindergartners and Second Graders." *Research in the Teaching of English* 22: 128–60.

12. Nicholson, T. 1997. "Closing the Gap on Reading Failure: Social Background, Phonemic Awareness, and Learning to Read." In *Foundation of Reading Aquisition and Dyslexia,* ed. B. A. Blachman, 381–408. Mahwah, NJ: Lawrence Erlbaum Associates.

13. Nicholson. "Closing the Gap." (Quotations on p. 384.)

14. Nicholson. "Closing the Gap." (Quotations on p. 386.)

15. Sahagun, L. 1998. "Facing the Poverty." *Los Angeles Times,* 1 November.

16. Wallach et al. "Poor Children." (Quotations on pp. 36, 38–39.)

17. Adams. *Beginning to Read.* (Quotations on p. 90.)

18. Lonigan et al. "Phonological Sensitivity." (Quotations on p. 308.)

19. Bowey. "Socioeconomic Status Differences." (Quotations on p. 485.)

20. Nicholson. "Closing the Gap." (Quotations on pp. 389, 401.)

Chapter 10

1. Stanovich, K. E. 1993/1994. "Romance and Reality." *Reading Teacher* 47 (December/January): 280–91. (Quotation on pp. 285–86.)

2. Lyon, G. R., and E. J. Kameenui. 1997. National Institute of Child Health and Human Development (NICHD) Research Supports the America Reads Challenge. <www.ed.gov/inits/americareads/nichd/html>.

3. Blachman, B. 1996. "Preventing Early Reading Failure." In *Learning Disability: Lifelong Issues,* ed. S. Cramer and W. Ellis. Quoted in Fletcher, J. M., and G. R. Lyon. "Reading: A Research-Based Approach." In *What's Gone Wrong in America's Classrooms,* ed. W. M. Evers. Stanford: Hoover Institution Press. (Quotations on p. 56.)

4. Taylor, D. 1998. *Beginning to Read and the Spin Doctors of Science.* Urbana, IL: National Council of Teachers of English. (Quotation on p. 184.)

5. Lyon, G. R. 1997. Testimony of G. Reid Lyon on Children's Literacy. Committee on Education and the Workforce, U.S. House of Representatives, Washington, D.C.; Lyon, G. R. 1996. "Why Johnny Can't Decode." *Washington Post,* 27 October.

6. Foorman, B. 1999. "Research and Hyperbole." Letter. *Education Week,* 13 January.

7. Foorman. "Research and Hyperbole."

8. Texas Reading Initiative: <www.governor.state.tx.us/Reading/>.

9. Dubose, L. 1999. "Running on Empty: The Truth About George W. Bush's 'Compassionate Conservatism.'" *The Nation,* 26 April, 11–17. (Quotations on pp. 12–13.)

10. Levins, R., and R. Lewontin. 1985. *The Dialectical Biologist.* Cambridge, MA: Harvard University Press. (Quotations on pp. 206–207.)

11. Mills, C. W. 1959. *The Sociological Imagination.* New York: Oxford University Press. (Quotations on p. 78.)

12. Brown, P. G. 1999. "Science in Modern Life." *The Sciences* (January/February): 4. (Quotations on p. 4.)

13. Mills. *The Sociological Imagination.* (Quotation on p. 58, emphasis in original.)

14. Taylor. *Beginning to Read.*

15. American Psychological Association. 1997. APA Publication Rights Form. Washington, D.C.: American Psychological Association.

16. Fletcher, J. 1998. Internet post on the National Reading Conference listserv. 27 March.

17. Foorman, B. 1998. Personal communication. 25 May.

Index